THE RUFFED GROUSE

THE RUFFED GROUSE

GORDON GULLION

PHOTOGRAPHS BY
TOM MARTINSON

NorthWord
PRESS, INC

The author wishes to acknowledge the New
York State Department of Environmental Con-
servation for permission to excerpt from the
book, *Ruffed Grouse: Life History - Propagation
- Management,* by Gardiner Bump, Robert W.
Darrow, Frank C. Edminster and Walter Cris-
sey, published in 1947. Acknowledgements
also to Charles Scribner's Sons for the Aldo
Leopold specified quote (pp. 131) from *Game
Management.* Copyright 1933 Charles Scrib-
ner's Sons. Renewed copyright 1961 Estella B.
Leopold. Reprinted with permission of Charles
Scribner's Sons.

Published as Paper No. 13,980 of the Miscel-
laneous series of the Minnesota Agricultural
Experiment Station on research conducted
under Minnesota Agricultural Experiment
Station Project No. 83H, supported by Hatch
Act funds.

Originally published as *Grouse of the North
Shore* by Willow Creek Press

NorthWord Press, Inc.
P.O. Box 1360
Minocqua, WI 54548

For a Free Catalog describing NorthWord's
line of nature books and gifts, call 1-800-
336-5666.

ISBN 1-55971-012-8

PREFACE

This book represents a fortunate combining of two opportunities. Tom Martinson, living on Minnesota's North Shore of Lake Superior, found a group of relatively docile ruffed grouse. Without concealment, he was able to follow these birds through the year obtaining an unparalleled collection of photographs of wild ruffed grouse as they went through their daily routines in the various seasons. A "labor of love" for Tom, he was particularly successful in recording the feeding and roosting activities of these grouse.

This book is based on a long study of ruffed grouse biology and management. The study, basically an examination of how these birds are affected by forest-management activities, has been underway for more than a quarter of a century. It is based at the Cloquet Forestry Center, a University of Minnesota College of Forestry instructional and research facility 21 miles west of the west end of Lake Superior. While not actually on the North Shore, the Cloquet Forest is only 72 miles from the area where Tom Martinson found his cooperative grouse. The important aspects of both the physical environment and habitat are similar on the two areas.

The Cloquet Forest Wildlife Project has been supported for its duration by the Agricultural Experiment Station of the University of Min-

nesota, St. Paul, with additional support from the Minnesota Department of Natural Resources, and in recent years by The Ruffed Grouse Society and James O. Matschulat of New York.

The data from the Cloquet project represents the efforts of at least 278 individuals. For a number of years, this project was under the direction of Dr. William H. Marshall. In addition, 11 graduate students, 199 forestry students, and 68 interns and others have participated in this work.

The Cloquet project, with support from the National Science Foundation, pioneered in the development of radio-telemetry techniques for monitoring the movements and behavior of free-living wild animals. When male ruffed grouse number 900 was released on the Cloquet Forest carrying a miniature radio transmitter on April 29, 1960, a milestone in wildlife research was passed. Radio-tracking techniques developed on this project over the next five years are still the prevalent method used in radio-telemetry studies a quarter-century later.

Mr. Sidney Markusen of Esko, Minnesota, who died in December 1983, played an especially significant role in the development of miniature radio-transmitters and the equipment used for radio-tracking wildlife.

While the setting for this story is the scenic North Shore of Lake Superior in Minnesota, this does not represent provincialism. The North Shore area is typical of by far the greatest extent of the continent-wide range of the ruffed grouse.

In choosing the photographs to be used in this book, we have often purposely chosen those that show how well ruffed grouse are concealed in their habitat. Our intent is to describe how these birds survive in the "real world." The real world for ruffed grouse is full of hazards and dense vegetation. Ruffed grouse spending much time in the open where they are easily photographed are generally short-lived birds.

Since I have believed for over 20 years that ruffed grouse have a unique relationship with the aspens, this association will be emphasized throughout the text. I believe it is no coincidence that the range of the ruffed grouse, which has the widest distribution of any resident game bird on the continent, corresponds very closely to the range of the aspens in North America. The two species of aspen, quaking and big-toothed, occur in over 26 percent of North America's forests, and quaking aspen has the third-widest distribution of any tree on earth.

Although a relationship between aspen and ruffed grouse was recognized nearly a century ago in both Maine and Oregon [54,70], it has only been in the past 20 years of research in northern Minnesota that this relationship has been investigated in detail and it's importance begun to be understood.

The text does not represent a thorough and comprehensive review of the literature concerning ruffed grouse; rather, it discusses what I believe to be the most important factors influencing these birds, together with some aspects of their biology which I feel are particularly interesting. While most of the information is derived from the Cloquet studies, I have drawn upon other sources when I felt certain points needed more documentation. In particular, I have used material from several graduate degree theses concerning ruffed grouse. These works contain much information that otherwise may never see publication -- there have been nine from the Cloquet Project alone. Whenever information from another source has been used, it is noted and the reference listed in the Bibliography.

A list of the scientific names of the plants and animals mentioned in the text is appended.

GORDON GULLION
CLOQUET
WINTER 1984

Tom and I want to acknowledge the role that two very important people have played in the development of this book. Had we not had the support and assistance of our patient wives, Jan Martinson and Ardelle "Vicki" Gullion, publication of this book would never have been realized.

Contents

Chapter One

THIS BIRD WE CALL RUFFED GROUSE

Before I talk about how ruffed grouse live on the North Shore of Lake Superior and elsewhere, I would like to develop a background concerning this bird.

It was named a ruffed grouse by the first European zoologists interested in providing standardized names for animals. This name was chosen to recognize the unique group of specialized feathers around the neck that can be erected to form a conspicuous ruff when the bird is excited. The native Ojibway Indians call this bird "benai."

Ruffed grouse are considered unique among birds, and zoologists placed them in the genus *Bonasa,* with only two other birds, the Eurasian hazel grouse, and the black-breasted hazel grouse. Our species, *umbellus,* is a resident in 39 states and all the Canadian provinces. The Eurasian *bonasia* ranges from southern France and Scandinavia eastward to Japan and Manchuria. The species *sewerzowi* lives in the mountains of western China. These three grouse, together with 13 other species divided into six genera, constitute the avian family Tetraonidae, living in the subaractic and temperate portions of the Northern Hemisphere [40].

This family, together with six other families, including the Phasianidae (New World quails,

Old World partridges, pheasants, chickens, and pea-fowl), and Meleagrididae (wild turkey), are lumped into a larger group of chicken-like birds, the order Galliformes. They all have certain basic similarities which indicate a common ancestor many millions of years ago.

Ruffed grouse have been in North America for a long time. Fossil remains of this species have been found in Pleistocene deposits in Maryland, Pennsylvania, Tennessee and California [11]. Dr. Paul Johnsgard believes ruffed grouse evolved in North America over a span of several million years from the same ancestral stock as the ptarmigans, which in turn descended from a more primitive grouse-like bird that lived in the Lower Miocene more than 12 million years ago [39].

The other grouse in North America range from the large sage grouse of the arid, Western sagebrush basins to the small, white-tailed ptarmigan living near timberline in the Western mountains. Included are the blue, Franklin's, and spruce grouse, most closely associated with Western and Northern coniferous (evergreen) forests; the prairie-chicken and sharp-tailed grouse of Midwestern grasslands; and the willow and rock ptarmigans of the treeless Arctic regions.

Weighing from 17.3 to 22.9 oz., ruffed grouse

Grouse living on the North Shore have been assigned to the race togata, *the St. Lawrence ruffed grouse.*

Tail colors can range from a clear silvery-gray to chestnut colored red phase. About 30 different color variations are recognized among Minnesota ruffed grouse alone.

are smaller than the sage, blue, pinnated, and sharptailed grouse, but larger than the spruce grouse and both the rock and white-tailed ptarmigans. Ruffed grouse and willow ptarmigan are about the same size.

Three grouse have a broad range across northern Eurasia. These include the large capercaillie, filling the niche in Old World forests that the blue and spruce grouse occupy on this continent; the black grouse living in habitats similar to those of our sharptail; and the hazel grouse, which lives in the same type of coverts occupied by ruffed grouse on this continent. Photographs of good hazel grouse habitat in eastern Siberia could have been taken in good ruffed grouse habitat in northern Minnesota, Michigan, Vermont, or Utah [6].

Both the willow and rock ptarmigan are circumpolar in their Arctic range, and both occur on the British Isles. The willow ptarmigan in Britain does not turn white in winter, as they do everywhere else. There they are called "red grouse."

In North America, the ruffed grouse species has been divided into several geographic races, or subspecies. Currently, 12 races are recognized, based mostly upon differences in coloration [1]. The grouse living on the North Shore in Minnesota have been assigned to the race **togata**, the St. Lawrence ruffed grouse.

Male and female ruffed grouse look very much alike, and don't have the obvious plumage differences that make it easy for a person to tell the sex of some other birds like pheasants or mallards. But there are some subtle plumage dif-

Tail feathers on an individual grouse are as unique to that bird as fingerprints to a human. Even feathers replaced following molting are nearly exact copies of the former ones.

A cock ruffed grouse. Relative to total body size, the tails of hens are consistently shorter than tails of cocks.

ferences. Most obvious is a difference in the length of the neck-ruff feathers, and there are some differences in tail feathers.

In relation to total body size, the tails of hens are consistently shorter than the tails of cocks. Among ruffed grouse in northern Minnesota, if the length of the central tail feathers is less than 5-5/8th inches, the bird is surely a hen, but if those feathers are longer than 5-15/16th inches, the bird is surely a cock. If the feather lengths are between these dimensions, depending upon age, it may be either sex.

Another characteristic becoming widely used to distinguish between male and female ruffed grouse is a difference in the number of white spots on the rump feathers [63]. If the correct feathers are examined and there are two or three spots present, the bird is probably a male, but if there is only one, or no spots, the bird is probably a female. The difficulty with this procedure lies in selecting the proper feathers for the spot count, for males also have rump feathers with one or no spots. One has to be careful to select rump feathers having the largest number of spots.

When someone is wondering about the sex of a dead grouse in the hand, the surest way is to open the body cavity and find the reproductive organs, or gonads. When a grouse with its intestines removed is laid on its back, two pinkish-brown organs about 1-1/2 inches long are evident on either side of the spinal column. These are the paired kidneys, and the gonads are at the head-end of the kidneys.

If the bird is a hen, the ovary looks like a clump of very small white grapes, about 1/4 to

Older males will either slip quietly off a drumming log and run before a threat nears, or remain motionless on the log if they believe the danger will pass no closer than 50 to 60 feet.

1/2 inch long, on the left side. The testes of the male are paired, one at the head of each kidney. A testis looks like a short piece of pencil lead in young males, and small, bean-shaped, and grayish in an adult. Each testis is sort of nestled on a yellowish adrenal gland, and you must be sure that it is the testes and not that gland you are examining.

Ruffed grouse elsewhere differ somewhat in size from the birds living in Minnesota. In Michigan, for example, young birds with tails 5-1/4th inches or less are females, and those with tails 5-3/8th inches or larger are males. Among adults, hens had tails 5-3/8th inches or shorter, and males 5-1/2 inches or longer [2]. In southeastern Ohio, females may have tails as long as 6-1/2 inches, and the tails of males may be as long as 7-7/8th inches [13]. In western Washington, there is much more overlap in tail lengths than occurs elsewhere, with both males and females having tails less than 6-1/8th inches, but only males have longer tails [9].

There can be a problem when tail lengths are used to determine the sex of ruffed grouse in the spring and summer. If the bird lost tail feathers

in a close encounter with a predator during the winter, the new feathers grown in replacement will be somewhat shorter. They may even have a different color tone than the feathers grown during normal summer replacement. There may be nearly an inch difference between the length of a regrown tail and that bird's normal tail. Sometimes these replacement tails are short enough that an inexperienced person might classify them as coming from a female.

These records of "near misses" are useful indicators of the year-to-year variations in the intensity of predator pressure. At Cloquet in the spring of 1975, for example, 10 of 60 drumming males handled had clearly escaped a close encounter with a predator. Some other years with a high incidence of "escapes" were 1972, with eight of 104 having shortened tails, in 1974 this occurred for seven of 54 birds, and in 1977, affected seven among 76 drummers [28]. For both grouse and predator, those near misses must be exciting indeed.

RUFFED GROUSE COME IN SEVERAL COLORS

As elsewhere across the primary range of ruffed grouse, these birds occur in several color phases. Most of the color variation is expressed in the tail, but there is also some variation in general plumage coloration. Some birds are gray all over, while others are quite brown. Tail colors can range from a clear silver-gray to a chestnut-colored red phase. About 30 different color variations are currently recognized among Minnesota ruffed grouse.

Most often, ruffed grouse elsewhere have been classed simply as gray- or red-phased, or sometimes gray, red, or intermediate-phased [32]. Some people talking about the red-phased grouse are actually referring to the color of the tail band, not the entire tail.

We recognize four distinct color phases or groups among Minnesota's male ruffed grouse, and most of these are replicated elsewhere. Although most birds fall clearly into one group or another, there are always a few borderline birds.

I feel that, with few exceptions, a grouse in flight is a grouse in trouble. The hazards of flight, including predation and accidental death, usually outweigh the advantages.

The silver-gray should have pure gray feathers, without any suggestion of brown or chestnut; the intermediate-gray is basically gray but with a varying suffusion of brown or chestnut; the brown is clearly a brown feather with prominent alternating light and dark transverse bars; the red-phase is the chestnut-colored tail with a single dark transverse bar, but lacking the light bar typical of the brown birds. This difference between the red and brown phases is partly the difference between the feathers having a single or double transverse bar [48].

The color of the subterminal band near the end of the tail is distinct from the general tail color. This band may be either black or bronze colored (or "red"). Black predominates, and the frequency of the bronze or reddish band varies. For example, among red-phased grouse in Minnesota, about one in eight will have the bronze band, and among the fairly rare brown-phased birds, about one in five will be bronze-banded. By contrast, bronze-colored bands occur in about one in nine silver-gray grouse and in one in six among intermediate-grays. But this, too, varies across the state. On the North Shore, the bronze band occurs in only one bird in 12.2, all colors combined, while in the southeastern corner of Minnesota, bronze occurs in one in 5.2 birds of all colors. The ruff feathers are always the same color as the tail band.

In the illustration showing ruffed grouse tails, the color variations shown, in clockwise order, are: red-phase with bronze band; red-phase with black band; intermediate-gray with bronze band; silver-gray (an especially dark one) with black band; brown-phase with a black band; and the most striking of all, a brown-phase with a bronze band. The number of color variations, when the tail band is included, number about 60 distinct, recurring color variations.

On the North Shore, 27.3 percent of the grouse are red, 37.6 percent are intermediate grays, with 25.1 and 10.0 percent in the silver-gray and brown phases respectively. This is in contrast to percentages of 30.4, 28.0, 28.0, and 13.6 respectively for those same colors in northwestern Minnesota, and 43.9, 16.8, 9.9 and 29.4 in southeastern Minnesota.

There are also some sex-related differences in tail colors and patterns. A uniformity of tail color

*The Boundary Waters Canoe Area has one
of the sparsest grouse populations in the
Great Lakes region . . .*

. . . except in those areas where wildfires have recreated livable habitats for fire-dependent wildlife species.

Cow moose with calf.
Snowshoe hare — summer phase.

Forest openings created by wildfire "hotspots" produce fleshy-leaved, herbaceous plants including raspberry and blueberry.

Generally, grouse reach "cyclic" population highs only in those areas where aspens are available to them.

is characteristic of males and red-phased females; that is, the two central feathers tend to be of the same color and pattern as the lateral feathers to either side. This is not true of "non-red" hens. Among the females, whose tails would be similar to the gray and brown phases of males, the central feathers are usually markedly redder than the adjacent lateral feathers. Sometimes the central feathers are so red that a gray-phased hen would be classified red-phased if only the central feathers were examined. The birds with dimorphic tails are called "split-phase," and this is a pattern unique to females. But interestingly, this appears to be a color pattern typical of both male

and female gray-phased hazel grouse in the Old World.

Color-phases are of more than academic interest, for the genetically determined tail color has some bearing on how long a grouse may live in northern Minnesota. Brown-phased grouse consistently have the shortest life span, while the red-phased birds tend to live longest.

Based on records of 950 male grouse from their first spring as an occupant of a drumming log to their deaths, we find brown-phased males have a mean survival of 11.3 months. Silver-gray birds are next shortest in longevity, at 12.8 months, while the intermediate-gray male grouse live an average of 14.6 months. Red-phased birds have a mean longevity of 15.3 months. Keep in mind that these figures reflect longevity of birds that have already survived their first 10 months when mortality rates are highest.

Since the numbers of adult hens and cocks remain nearly equal in the population each fall and winter, it seems apparent that there is not much difference in mortality rates. Adult males suffer accelerated losses during the spring and fall drumming seasons, while a greater toll of hens is taken through the summer while they are nesting and rearing their broods.

We don't understand why, but the more severe the climate, the greater the loss among red-phased ruffed grouse. In northern Minnesota, fewer red-phased grouse survive than grayish birds during those winters when snow cover is unfavorable and the temperatures bitterly cold [26]. Following more favorable winters, the proportion of red birds in the population increases. As the proportions of red-phased grouse in the population wax and wane, so does the overall abundance of ruffed grouse. The numbers of gray birds seem to stay fairly constant, and when they constitute the dominant color-phase, ruffed grouse tend to be relatively scarce. When red-phased grouse prosper, overall abundance increases, and we have a "cyclic" high.

CONSPICUOUS ABSENCES OF RUFFED GROUSE IN MAJOR ASPEN AREAS

While there is a close relationship between the primary range of ruffed grouse and the aspens, especially quaking aspen, there is a puzzling absence of ruffed grouse from two major aspen areas in North America.

The largest area is in the central Rocky Mountains, from the Medicine Bow Mountains in southeastern Wyoming, south through Colorado to the mountains of northern Arizona and New Mexico. There are some 2.72 million acres of aspen forests in this region, but no positive evidence of ruffed grouse, either past or present [36]. There are supposed records of ruffed grouse in this region, but no specimens or even feathers exist to support the records. My personal experience in that region strongly suggests that these records were based on misidentifications of immature blue grouse.

Having examined aspen habitats in all parts of southeastern Wyoming and Colorado, and some parts of east-central Arizona (White Mountains) and northern New Mexico, there appears to be a great deal of suitable habitat there for ruffed grouse. At least these habitats appear to have all the components of coverts occupied by ruffed grouse farther west in the Wasatch and Uinta Ranges in Utah, and the Bighorn and Wind River Ranges farther north in Wyoming.

Ruffed grouse, being weak-flighted, have apparently never crossed the Red Desert of south-central Wyoming or the Green River drainage of eastern Utah. This is not surprising, for they failed to naturally cross the 10-mile-wide Strait of Belle Isle which separates Newfoundland from the mainland, or the 16 miles from the North Shore of Lake Superior to Isle Royale, a flight that sharp-tailed grouse did make.

Ruffed grouse are also absent from the high Sierra Nevada in central California. Although ruffs do occur along the Humboldt Coast in northwestern California, in habitats contiguous with ruffed grouse range farther north in Oregon, they evidently failed to cross the high lava plateau country between the southern end of the Cascades in Oregon and the high aspen country more than 100 miles farther south in the Sierras. I am not very familiar with that country, but being familiar with the habitats where ruffed grouse have become successfully established in northeastern Nevada, I suspect the high Sierra aspen forests would sustain a ruffed grouse population, too.

From 1,000 eggs laid, about 262 young
grouse reach full size in September. Of these,
roughly 118 will survive to participate in
spring breeding activities.

There are differences in the relative frequency of these color-phases across North America [32]. In the far north, where winters are even more bitter than on the North Shore, most of the ruffed grouse are gray-phased. In the Yukon Valley of Alaska, only about one grouse in four is a red bird. Farther south, as the climate moderates, the proportion of red birds in the resident grouse population increases. In the mild maritime climate on Vancouver Island, British Columbia, about 75 percent of the grouse are red-phased. Still farther south on the Olympic Peninsula in western Washington, the gray phase is rare, if it occurs at all. Throughout the forested country west of the Cascade Range in Washington, Oregon, and northwestern California, most ruffed grouse are a dark, red-phase.

In the colder climates east of the Cascades in Oregon and Washington, gray birds become an important component of ruffed grouse populations. The color-phase ratios, and colors that we have seen in a sample of tails from Idaho, Montana, Utah, and Wyoming are similar to those from Minnesota.

In the central part of the continent, the ruffed grouse population is increasingly dominated by the red-phased form as one moves south. Among a sample of 736 ruffs from Alberta, Canada, 58 percent were gray-phased, 19 percent intermediate, and 31 percent reds [1]. In Ohio, the red-phase is clearly dominant in all but the northeastern part of the state, and all of the ruffed grouse in Kentucky and Tennessee are red birds. The native ruffed grouse in Missouri and south into Arkansas was red-phased.

In New England, both the red- and gray-phases are present, and all of the tails we have seen from that region are similar to Minnesota colors. In Maine, some people call the gray birds from the conifer-forested northern parts of the state the "spruce partridge" (different than the "fool-hen" or spruce grouse). The red-phase grouse living in Maine's hardwood forests nearer the coast are called "birch partridges."

Farther south on the East Coast, the red-phase becomes increasingly prevalent. The ruffed grouse in central New York, where Dr. Gardiner Bump and his associates studied these birds in the 1930s, were all red-phased [12], and most of the ruffed grouse in Pennsylvania are red birds. This pattern seems to prevail along the Appalachian Mountains as far south as northern Georgia [48]. However, even in the southern Appalachians, gray-phased ruffed grouse occur among the red spruces at higher elevations where the climate is cooler and more Canadian-like.

In a recent continent-wide study of ruffed grouse color-phases, Bruce Lawson concluded that the prevalence of the various colors is related partly to temperature regimens with some relationship to prevailing humidity conditions [48].

The closely-related Old World's hazel grouse also occurs as a gray and a reddish phase. Like our bird, the gray-phase is more common in the colder, northern parts of its range, while the reddish birds become more numerous farther south in warmer climates [59].

In northern Minnesota, intensity of raptor predation influences the color-phase composition of the ruffed grouse population. When goshawks nested on the Cloquet Forest from 1956 to 1967, red-phased grouse had a significantly shorter life span than gray-phased birds in the same forest [32]. Red-phased birds were also a minority in the population. During the absence of nesting goshawks at Cloquet from 1968 to 1977, the proportion of red birds increased to as much as 55

*Aspens often grow as clones with massive,
inter-connecting root systems that produce
suckers after standing trees are removed.
All trees in a clone are of like sex.*

percent of the population, and longevity of the red-phased males exceeded that of gray-phased males. After goshawks resumed nesting on the Cloquet Forest in 1978, the proportion of red birds declined to less than 40 percent, and survival of red males dropped well below that of gray-tailed males [29].

RUFFED GROUSE ARE NOT PARTRIDGES!

The exhortations of a multitude of hunters notwithstanding, ruffed grouse are about as similar to partridges as goats are to moose. Our bird is a native, thriving in deep snow and cold winters, feeding primarily on the leaves, buds, and fruits of trees and shrubs.

Partridges, on the other hand, are native to the Old World, feeding primarily on seeds and grains, and are much less tolerant of snow. Two species of Old World partridges, the gray and chukar, are established as "exotics" in North America. The gray partridge, sometimes called the Hungarian partridge, or "Hun," is a widespread game bird in agricultural areas in western and southern Minnesota and elsewhere in the Midwest. The chukar is well established on overgrazed or frequently-burned rangelands in the more arid Western regions, especially in the Great Basin portions of Idaho, Oregon, Nevada, and Utah. For many years, a small population of chukars persisted on an iron-mine dump near Ely, in northern Minnesota.

RUFFED GROUSE ARE SOLITARY BIRDS

There are some other important differences among ruffed grouse, the quails and partridges, and many other birds. Our bird tends to be a social "loner," seldom associating with other grouse in a structured covey or flock. When several ruffed grouse find a food supply or some other condition mutually attractive, they collect briefly to share the bounty. But once the sharing has ended, the birds go their separate ways.

Each ruffed grouse is responsible for its own welfare and survival. Among the coveying quails and partridges, the alarm of a single individual is enough to trigger an escape response by the entire group; they act as a cohesive, social unit. This is not true of ruffed grouse. Each one, even when in a group, assesses the situation and responds according to its own evaluation of the danger.

This is clearly to the advantage of grouse hunters, for it often gives them several shooting opportunities when they get into a group of ruffed grouse, as each flushes independently of the others.

There is also a marked difference in how grouse of different ages respond to disturbance. Young, inexperienced ruffed grouse have to learn to respond wisely, but most of them die before they learn. When approached, a young grouse is often uncertain about how to respond. Its tendency is to stay put, hoping to be overlooked. When approached too closely, it becomes nervous and flushes. On the other hand, grouse that survive have learned to run well ahead of an approaching hunter, to move well off to one side of the projected path of approach, and then to sit tight as they are passed by. This is why the number of young grouse in the hunter's bag each fall is not very representative of the true ratios of young to adult grouse in the population.

This differential behavior is particularly evident among drumming males. It is the young male on a drumming log that can be approached more closely, and he'll usually fly when he feels threatened. Older males either quietly slip off the log and run before a potential threat gets near them, or remain motionless on a log if they believe they'll be passed by 50 to 60 feet to one side.

Generally, considering a bird's ability to fly, we think of easy and rapid mobility. Distance seems to be of little consequence, and there appears to be few limitations upon a grouse's ability to utilize assorted habitat resources scattered over a wide area.

Certainly the sudden burst from cover by a flushing ruffed grouse, which can be startling to someone stalking these birds, suggests that the bird is indeed launching into a flight that should take it at least into the next county, if not the next state. But no, this is one of the deceptions these birds thrive upon. For ruffed grouse are not a highly mobile species, and each bird usually spends its life within a comparatively small area.

Flight appears to be a safe way to move from one point to another, especially as a quick means of escape. But for a bird living in dense forest cover, is flight all that much of an advantage? Obviously, the answer is "yes" when the snow is deep and soft, and the only food is on the twigs of shrubs and trees overhead. But at other times, the hazards associated with flight may outweigh its advantages. Aside from the very high energy costs, I believe flying "ruffs" also greatly increase their chances for either accidental death or predation.

In the fall of 1979, I examined a hen that had hit a pine branch in the headquarters area of the Cloquet Forestry Center. She hit that branch with such force that the bones in the pectoral girdle supporting the wing on the right side were almost pulverized, some of the muscles in her breast were torn loose from the sternum, and a pulmonary artery had ruptured, filling one lung with blood.

I have gradually developed the feeling that a grouse in flight is usually a grouse in trouble, except for the wintertime flights up into trees and bushes and back to a snow roost.

RUFFED GROUSE NEED DISTURBED FORESTS

Ruffed grouse on the North Shore are living in the typical range of this species. But in northeastern Minnesota, they are existing in some of the poorer habitat within their range. Even though people are relatively scarce on Minnesota's North Shore, so are ruffed grouse. The statewide roadside drumming counts made by Minnesota's wildlife managers and U.S. Forest Service personnel each spring consistently show the North Shore grouse population to number one-third to one-quarter that of other parts of the state [46]. Much of the North Shore remains virtual wilderness. In our time, wilderness usually means soils too poor and a climate too severe for farming. Wilderness also implies a lack of forest disturbance. These two factors -- poor soils and lack of forest disturbance -- predicate a relatively sparse population of ruffed grouse.

The Boundary Waters Canoe Area, a

HABITAT QUALITY AND SOCIAL TOLERANCE LIMIT GROUSE DENSITIES

The information about relative ruffed grouse densities, and even of dispersion, tells us something of importance. That is, when the habitat is really suitable for these birds, and has the food and cover resources they require, breeding ruffed grouse should be quite evenly spaced throughout woody cover about 150 yards apart at densities approximating 10 breeding pairs per 100 acres. This is the limit of their social tolerance. Above this density, intra-species competition limits the number of ruffed grouse. Conversely, if densities are much below this level, an inadequate habitat is indicated. This might be a consequence of poor distribution of cover or inadequate food resources. It is probably seldom that ruffed grouse coverts approach this quality over extensive areas, but at Cloquet we did have one tract of about 200 acres which sustained a population close to this density for 11 years.

1,030,000 acre wilderness adjacent to the North Shore area, probably has one of the sparsest ruffed grouse populations in the Great Lakes region, except where wildfires have recently renewed the forest and recreated livable habitats for a number of fire-dependent species of forest wildlife.

In the primeval forest, natural ecological agents such as fire and windstorm periodically destroyed the forest and stimulated renewal. A study of the fire history of the Boundary Waters Area by Dr. Miron Heinselman showed that major fires had burned many parts of the area about every 26 years over the past several hundred years [35]. He believed that nearly the entire area was burned at least once a century. This frequency of disturbance maintained a particularly rich ecosystem, an association of plants and animals that requires frequent renewal. The system is dominated by the aspens and a number of other plant species that cannot tolerate shade, needing full sunlight to grow.

More recently, logging has replaced wildfire as the primary method by which these forests can be maintained as productive wildlife habitats. Logging usually fails to provide some of the benefits to wildlife that fire provides, but it is a lot more acceptable to modern society.

Ruffed grouse are just one of a number of wildlife species which are dependent upon periodic forest disturbance. When one looks carefully at the aftermath of a wildfire in northern Minnesota, and follows the subsequent forest succession, one sees a natural sequence of coverts providing different qualities of habitats at different times.

If the fire has burned an area where a network of aspen roots lies near the surface of the soil, a profusion of rapidly-growing suckers will develop. During the first season following fire or logging, these suckers grow at rates exceeding an inch a day at densities approaching a sucker per square foot.

After three or four years, these root suckers often reach heights of eight to 12 feet and begin providing the best possible habitat for a ruffed grouse hen with her brood. The birds have a relatively clean forest floor where there is a minimum likelihood of foxes, bobcats, or skunks finding the concealment that allows them to ambush the brood. The canopy is closed overhead, preventing attack by hawks or owls, collectively called "raptors."

In any forest fire, there are occasional spots where the heat is so intense that tree roots and seeds are destroyed. In those places, a profusion of fleshy-leafed, herbaceous plants usually develops, including strawberries, blueberries, and other fruit producers. These are the openings where the woodland sedges are most likely to bear fruit. The seeds of quite a number of forest plants need to be exposed to fire before they will germinate. Some other seeds simply need to be exposed to the unshaded heat of the summer sun to germinate. Openings created by a fire "hotspot" are usually a few feet or a few yards across and not large enough to create an "ecological trap" for grouse. This is in contrast to the vulnerability to predation a brood faces by coming out into larger openings such as trails or roadways.

Ruffed grouse prosper best in a very dynamic forest ecosystem, one that undergoes continuous change over a period of 30 years. They use the differently-aged stages of this forest for different purposes.

The aspen stand developing in secondary succession goes through a series of natural events which maintain it as a continually valuable wildlife habitat. The first two years of development typically consists of a sucker stand having densities which may reach or exceed 70,000 stems per acre. Within three or four years, many of the slower-growing trees die as they lose the race to stay in sunlight, and natural thinning begins. Grouse broods begin using this type of cover. By the time the stand is eight to 10 years old, it has usually thinned to a density of six to eight thousand stems per acre. This is the stage when adult ruffed grouse begin using these stands extensively as fall, winter, and spring cover. The stand then has another period of rapid growth, but stagnates at between 15 to 20 years of age and undergoes another period of thinning which usually reduces stem densities by about one-half. Because of reduced competition, this is followed by another growth period, then stagnation and thinning that reduces the stand to less than 2,000 stems per acre at 25 to 30 years of age. This last thinning usually establishes the final density of the mature aspen stand 30.

At this stage, the density is below that which ruffed grouse find acceptable, and it has "gone-by" as grouse cover. But mature aspen this age produce the flower buds used for winter food and the catkins that are so important to grouse in the spring. If the aspen stand is not destroyed and regenerated in another 10 to 20 years, it becomes decadent, with heart-rot frequent. Then "breakup" commences when the trees and their roots begin to die, and aspen is eventually lost from the site. The forest type moves on to another stage dominated by tree species not as valuable to ruffed grouse.

RUFFED GROUSE DO BEST IN A SPECIFIC HABITAT

Due to their widespread distribution across North America, from coast to coast, and from the sub-Arctic to the hills of Georgia and Arkansas, ruffed grouse have often been considered to be a highly-adaptable species. But that is not really true. The habitat niches they occupy do not vary much from the northwest coast of California to the Yukon Valley, nor from the Wasatch Mountains of Utah to the Green Mountains of Vermont. Ruffed grouse have such a wide range because the specific habitat they depend upon is widely-distributed. But when ruffed grouse are outside the range of aspen, they are living in habitats which should be considered peripheral to their primary range.

In contrast to breeding densities that reach 20 grouse per 100 acres or more in good aspen habitats, ruffed grouse breeding densities seldom exceed two to four birds per 100 acres in those parts of their range remote from aspen forests.

To interpret this, four grouse per 100 acres means that a person would walk 2.1 miles to flush a single bird, assuming that it will flush at an average distance of 48 feet rather than run. At

a breeding density of 20 birds per 100 acres, a walk of only 0.4 miles should flush one grouse. Converting these breeding densities to the frequency at which hunters should encounter grouse in the fall, two pairs of breeding grouse in 100 acres should mean about a grouse per nine acres in the fall, and a walk of 0.8 miles to find one. At 20 breeding grouse (10 pairs) per 100 acres, the grouse per 1.8 acres would require only about 900 feet of walking to have a random flush. A dog that covers a great deal more country sure speeds the process of finding these birds, whatever the density.

But even in aspen-dominated forests, ruffed grouse will not reach the densities cited above unless there is an interspersion of young and old forest stands to provide the proper intermixture of needed food and cover.

In this discussion of grouse habitat and comparative densities, it should be pointed out that even in the heart of ruffed grouse range, where some of the highest densities occur, there are habitats devoid of grouse. The Cloquet Forest is a well-documented example of this. It has been a refuge since 1924, except for a four-weekend special hunt on one portion in 1961. Yet on this five-square-mile refuge, there are large tracts of forest that have been little used by grouse for as long as records have been maintained here. But nearby there are other tracts that have supported some of the highest densities recorded anywhere.

The problem is separating acceptable grouse habitat from those areas that are not. If we review ruffed grouse densities on the Cloquet Forest in 1972, for example, the gross density --that is, the total number of breeding males on the entire forest -- was only 3.9 males per 100 acres. But if we separate the areas that were little used, if at all, we find: 663 acres of lowland spruce-fir-cedar with four birds, for a density of 0.6 per 100 acres, and another 44 acres of 165 year-old virgin red pine forest that has been used by only one drummer that we know about in the past 50 years. From this gross area, we should eliminate the 200 acres of administrative areas, open fields, marshes, muskeg, and recently-logged areas that are not used by ruffed grouse.

Improved aspen management practices in the Great Lakes and northeastern forests are brightening the future for ruffed grouse.

There are also another 339 acres of upland and lowland brush and other habitats that are barren as far as ruffed grouse are concerned.

The forest where aspen is present among the dominant conifers includes 140 acres of upland balsam-fir and spruce forest, where grouse densities were 8.6 per 100 acres. Included here are 908 acres of high-tree pine stands where the 1972 density averaged 2.8 males per 100 acres. The 123 acres of young pine plantations had a density of 4.9 males per 100 acres. The 44 acres of lowland hardwood had a density of nine males per 100 acres. This leaves the 875 acres of predominately aspen and birch forests of various ages. There, the breeding male density was 9.1 birds per 100 acres. But in the aspen-birch type, the best densities, at 22 males per 100 acres, were in the 213 acres of 12 to 25 year-old aspen saplings -- a male for every four and-a-half acres. There are considerable differences in grouse densities that can be related to quality of habitat, even on a refuge in the heart of grouse country.

Another difference that density figures do not convey concerns the dispersion of birds in the habitat. In the best aspen sapling habitats, breeding males are quite evenly dispersed throughout the stand at predictable distances from one another. But in the other forest types this is not the case. In these poorer habitats, ruffed grouse tend to be clustered in areas where the habitat has some attributes not evenly distributed throughout the type. For example, in the high-tree pine type in 1972, there was one section where four males were quite evenly spaced through about 25 acres having an intermixture of aspen in the canopy and dense hazel cover in the understory. But another 658 acres of this type had no grouse present. So even in this type, densities expressed as gross acreage are misleading.

HOW LONG DO RUFFED GROUSE LIVE?

A frequently-asked question is: "How long do ruffed grouse live?" The answer first requires another question: "From when?" If we compute survival from the time the eggs are laid and incubation commences, about 32 percent of the eggs will be destroyed before they hatch. Of those hatching, about 60 percent of the chicks die before they are fully grown. From 1,000 eggs laid, about 262 young grouse reach full size in mid-September. On the average, and there are few average years, about 55 percent of the young birds will die between mid-September and the end of April, so about 118 should be alive to participate in breeding activity at the age of 11 months. From then on, annual survival averages about 45 percent from breeding season to breeding season, but may vary from as low as 30 percent in some years to as high as 66 percent in others. So usually about 49 birds from the original 1,000 eggs will be alive at the start of the second breeding season, 20 alive entering the third season, and 11 going into the fourth season. One ruffed grouse out of 1,000 eggs may reach the age of six. At Cloquet, we have had three out of over 1,300 banded male grouse that lived to be eight years old.

PERIODICALLY, RUFFED GROUSE BECOME SCARCE

A trait of ruffed grouse and some other animals that has long puzzled biologists and others has been the tendency for their numbers to vary periodically in the northern parts of their range [41]. These changes have been so regular and dramatic that they are called "cycles." There is roughly a 10-year interval between periods of peak ruffed grouse abundance.

The ruffed grouse cycles in northern Minnesota have a high degree of predictability. In each decade, periods of peak abundance have occurred in years ending in 0, 1, 2, or 3, and the bottom of the depression has been in one of the years ending in 4, 5, or 6. Grouse populations increase during years ending in 7 and 8, and decline in years ending in 3 or 4. At least, that is the way it's been since 1920.

With data now spanning 50 years at Cloquet, it appears that a 20-year cycle is superimposed upon the 10-year cycle, with especially high populations occurring in the early 1930's, 1950's, 1970's, and due to roll around in the 1990's.

WHY these periodic fluctuations occur has proven more difficult to explain. Since this cyclic phenomenon was first recognized, a number of theories have been advanced, each having some

relationship to environmental factors or how other animals interact with grouse. At least one theory ties grouse cycles to sunspots and another to the lunar cycle. But there seem to be flaws in all of the theories developed so far, and we are still unsure of the underlying causes.

We can say with some confidence that recreational hunting each fall does not seem to be one of the factors involved in lowering ruffed grouse numbers, even when populations are at a cyclic low.

Generally, it is only in the regions where ruffed grouse have aspen available that these birds periodically reach levels of great abundance -- the cyclic highs. In northern regions, when grouse are scarce, their numbers are approximately equal to the density of grouse found on the periphery of their range where aspen is not a part of their habitat. The difference between abundance and scarcity in these northern regions is a factor of five to 10 times.

In more southern areas, outside the area where aspen is important, the fluctuations are less evident, but grouse tend to persist at lower levels of abundance.

Later, in the chapter on foods and feeding behavior, I'll discuss another possible explanation of why these periodic fluctuations occur.

HOW ARE THESE THINGS LEARNED ABOUT GROUSE?

This is not a technical report, but we find that many persons are intrigued by the methods we use to collect the information that allows us to tell this story.

The development of the technique for tracking free-living grouse by saddling them with miniature radio-transmitters was noted in the Preface. This technique was used extensively on the Cloquet Project from 1960 to 1965, and much information concerning the movements and behavior of individual ruffed grouse was collected. Unfortunately, very little of this information has been published.

Both the radio-telemetry work and other information about individual ruffed grouse is based on birds that have been captured, banded, and released. The two primary methods used to trap grouse have been the "lily-pad" and the mirror traps.

The lily-pad trap is an 18-inch high welded-wire cage with a funnel-shaped entrance. It is similar to a "clover-leaf" trap developed a number of years ago for trapping shorebirds. Grouse are led into this trap by two-foot-high poultry wire fences, or "wings," extending 50 to 100 feed from the trap. Ruffed grouse usually walk along the fence, looking for a way through it rather than jumping over it, and stroll into the trap.

During the winter, the wings become useless as snow deepens, so we turn to another ruse to capture ruffed grouse. Although these birds normally do not feed on grains, we've found that if we dyed yellow-shelled corn red, orange, or purple, grouse would eat it. Evidently they believed they'd found an abundance of berries, and entered the traps to feed on the dyed corn.

The other method for capturing grouse is the mirror trap. This technique was originally developed by Glen Bowers and Dale Tanner in Pennsylvania and still is our best method for capturing males on their drumming logs. This is a box trap with a mirror in the back. When the drumming male stands on his log, proclaiming his superiority to all within hearing, he becomes antagonized by his image in the mirror. Believing his image to be a rival, he enters the trap to drive the intruder away.

At Cloquet we have captured about 34 percent of the male grouse the first time this trap was presented to them. Each year we handle 70 to 90 percent of the drumming males on the study area using this procedure.

Some of the 66 percent of the drummers we don't capture right away can prove very difficult to lure into a mirror trap. Some of these birds were trapped before and they are not inclined to be fooled again. These wise old males are among our longer-lived grouse. But one of our longest-lived, hot-tempered males was captured in a mirror trap each of the eight spring seasons that he used a drumming log!

The other group we have trouble capturing are the smaller males, particularly the small, adult birds that delayed their occupation of a drumming log. These small males are apparently so low in the social hierarchy and with such a low level of self-esteem that they are frightened by their own reflection in the mirror and temporarily abandon their log. However, if we leave the trap unset on the log long enough, most of them will eventually accept the "other" bird, and even begin roosting in the trap beside their image. Then, we reset the trap and capture him.

Grouse trapped on the Cloquet project are released carrying four colored-aluminum bands, two on each leg, in a unique, coded combination which allows us to identify the birds when we see them in the woods.

THE FUTURE LOOKS BRIGHT!

To close this chapter on an optimistic note, ruffed grouse seem to be one wildlife species with a bright future on this continent.

In the Great Lakes and Northeastern forests, the increasing commercial importance of aspen and improved management of aspen as a forest resource give particular reason for optimism concerning the future for ruffed grouse.

Timber-management practices are being modified to provide better habitat for ruffed grouse and other species of forest wildlife. These changes have resulted from long-term research which has provided a better understanding of what ruffed grouse need in the forest, how they can use it, and how it can be provided.

As the result of recent successful restocking in forested areas from which they disappeared earlier in this century, ruffed grouse currently occur in nearly every state where they were native in 1600 [31]. In addition, ruffed grouse have become established as non-native "exotics" in Newfoundland and Nevada through transplanting wild-trapped grouse from nearby areas. But much of their primeval forest habitat in the Midwest and some parts of the Great Lakes region has been converted to cropland or to other uses, so there they will never again be as abundant as they once were.

Chapter Two

SPRING

The chill of Lake Superior delays snow melting on the North Shore into late April, occasionally into May. Sometimes the big lake still has ice floes on it as late as early June, and that 27-mile-wide expanse of water, with a temperature just above freezing, allows winter to hold a grip on adjacent shores longer than surrounding areas. This effect is sufficient to allow several subarctic plants to thrive near the shoreline, hundreds of miles south of where they would usually be expected.

Even though the ground may still be in the grip of winter, ruffed grouse respond to a different regulator. They begin normal, springtime activities long before the weather says it's spring. Their commencement of breeding activity is governed by the length of day, and daily behavior is only locally affected by weather.

Although a foot or two of snow may still cover their drumming logs, male ruffed grouse begin visiting those sites frequently by the middle of March. Though the log was indistinguishable in the deep snow, we have seen occasions when the bird stood and drummed on the snow directly above the drumming stage he normally uses. This was done with such precision that as the snow melted, the droppings he left settled right onto the place where he normally drummed

when the log was bare.

Most male grouse are reluctant to drum as long as snow surrounds their logs, regardless of the stage of the season. This probably reflects an awareness that if they attract attention by drumming, and are stalked by a predator, they would be exceedingly vulnerable while escaping across a snow surface. A brown grouse moving across white snow is a conspicuous target for an alert, hungry predator already attracted by drumming.

The spring season for male ruffed grouse is primarily a season of defense and advertisement. The defensive activity is the protection of an area against the intrusion by other males. At the same time, he is advertising his readiness to breed and inviting the visits of hens to mate.

A male stays close to his drumming log at this season, seldom ranging more than 600 feet from his log. But there are records of individual males going on forays that took them as far as 3,000 feet from their drumming logs for a day or two [5]. Hens, on the other hand, may move one-half mile from where they spent the winter in response to the drumming of an established male [8].

Often there are a few males in the population that do not have drumming logs they can call their own [27]. Some of these males move around

Most males are reluctant to drum before snow melts from their immediate log area. A drumming grouse visible against a white backdrop makes a conspicuous target for predators.

looking for a vacant log, but this spring shuffle is of minor extent compared to fall dispersal and is relatively unimportant as far as the population is concerned -- that is, the spring mobility of these unattached males is too restricted to assure a replacement of other males that may have died late in the fall after dispersal has ended or during the winter. In the spring season, unattached male grouse seldom move as much as 1,000 feet from where they wintered.

This is a season of accelerated mortality. Snow can seldom be penetrated for roosting at this time of year, but it still lies nearly everywhere in the forest. Almost any grouse activity puts their dark bodies in sharp contrast to the white snow cover, both day and night. This is also the time when many of the raptors that moved south in the fall are moving back north to their nesting regions. These are not the clumsy, inept, young birds that harassed grouse in the fall; the raptors passing through in the spring are now experienced predators, not likely to let pursued prey escape.

Also, at this season, cover for ruffed grouse is the poorest of any time during the year. Protective foliage has long since fallen from the deciduous trees and shrubs. Even the bracken

fern, which provides concealment in many North Shore coverts until a heavy snowfall, has been crushed by the weight of the snow. All the things that provided concealment for ruffed grouse in the fall are now compressed into a layer a few inches thick on the forest floor. The birds have to depend upon their protective, or "cryptic," coloration to remain unseen and cover sufficiently dense to hamper the penetration by winged predators if they are sighted.

Food resources are also at a minimum in early spring. The flower buds and catkins growing in the more secure locations were taken by grouse earlier in the season. At this time of the year, the birds must feed in more exposed situations.

In early April, the male aspens begin flowering. Within a period of a few hours or a few days, the dormant aspen flower buds produce a long, caterpillar-like catkin which is a particularly choice food for ruffed grouse. Through April and into early May, both male and female grouse feed upon these catkins almost to the exclusion of any other food.

It is not until the male aspen flowers shed their pollen, dry up, and begin to fall from the trees that ruffed grouse turn to other food sources.

Spring drumming is governed by length of daylight hours, which means that along the North Shore male grouse are active on their logs long before spring-like weather arrives.

Early-spring cover for ruffed grouse is the poorest of the year. The birds must rely upon their cryptic coloration to remain unseen by winged predators.

Then they begin feeding heavily upon the leaves of frost-resistant, herbaceous plants, including strawberry, bunchberry, and gold thread. Also, as ferns begin to push their way through the leaf-mat on the forest floor, ruffed grouse find these succulent "fiddle-necks" particularly choice. Being the flower-eaters that they are, ruffed grouse pick the new blossoms of springbeauties and the other early-flowering plants.

The ruffed grouse hen selects her mate when she is ready for breeding and goes to the vicinity of his drumming log to accomplish the act. The hen moves to the vicinity of the log, gives the male of her choice the proper signs, and after a courtship that lasts only a few minutes -- no more than a few hours at best -- mating is accomplished.

The male grouse displaying to a hen near his drumming log is a sight to behold. His tail is spread to its fullest extent, his ruff is erected and sparkles with its iridescence; the combs over his eyes glow like fiery embers. His wings are rigidly drooped so the tips drag the ground; he is truly a

thing of splendor. As he struts before the hen, he stomps with each step, crunching the leaves underfoot, his ruff makes a rustling sound as he shakes his head. This display continues until the hen either loses interest and leaves, or becomes submissive, squats, and permits him to mount.

Greenup on the North Shore really begins in mid-May. The leaves of the earliest clones of aspen begin showing by the end of the first week in May to be followed by the birches, maples, and other hardwoods. The silvery leaves of the big-toothed aspen usually appear about two to three weeks after the leaves of the quakies. On the forest floor, the hepaticas, anemones, and trout lilies are among the earliest to flower, followed by strawberries, trailing-arbutus, and milkwort. Juneberry and blueberry begin flowering in mid-May, followed by the pin-cherries and then the chokecherries. About the time grouse nests are hatching, the false lily-of-the-valley and bunchberry are in flower. Summer greenery is fully developed by the first of June. Another noteworthy event in this country - mosquitoes start becoming obnoxious about May 15, give or take a few days.

Late spring is a busy season for all wildlife.

After food sources in appropriate cover have been exhausted, grouse must feed in more exposed situations.

The appetites of young goshawks can account for many grouse losses in spring. We once traced 11 banded birds to a single goshawk nest!

Whitetailed deer fawns are usually born in early June on the North Shore, and the young of other animals are growing rapidly. Of particular importance to ruffed grouse is the voracious appetite of young goshawks and horned owls. The parents of these young raptors are working long hours to find the food needed to keep these fuzzy youngsters growing. That means that ruffed grouse, snowshoe hares, red squirrels, crows, porcupines, flickers, and other prey species are dying frequently to provide this nourishment. At Cloquet in May, 1978, we knew that at least 11 banded ruffed grouse were brought to a nest containing two young goshawks over a two-week period.

Her tail braced against a branch for support, a hen grouse busily feeds upon aspen flower buds.

Chapter Three

DRUMMING

The distant drumming of the male ruffed grouse is, for many, synonymous with a wild forest. Fishermen working a favorite trout stream in the spring often hear the drummer's roll from nearby hillsides. Canoeists drifting down a river on a midsummer afternoon may hear an occasional drum from the bordering woodlands. In the fall, hunters waiting quietly for a wary whitetail frequently hear the distant drumming of the male ruffed grouse. Midwinter drumming is infrequent, but occurs from time to time. It is not often heard, but the unmistakable marks can be found on snow-covered logs in January and February.

Although the drumming of the male ruffed grouse is a year-round activity, it is most often heard as the snow melts in the spring and the breeding season approaches. Then anxious males are advertising their locations to hens looking for mates. At other times of the year, and probably even in the spring, the important function of drumming is territorial defense. This is the act of one male announcing to all the others within hearing that the particular forest area he is occupying is all his. He is defending an "activity center" against trespass by other males. The activity center is a small area in the immediate vicinity of one or several display sites, or "drumming logs." In contiguous, good ruffed grouse habitat, drumming males are often spaced quite evenly, about 148 to 159 yards apart, so that each bird dominates about eight to 10 acres of forest habitat. While each male attempts to maintain his activity center as an exclusive domain, areas farther away from his logs may be used by other males, but at different times.

Drumming logs and activity centers can be categorized based on the history of their use. While not all logs and centers fit neatly into one or another of these categories, most do, providing a convenient way to define these places when we are trying to determine their relative values to ruffed grouse.

First, the male grouse most frequently stands at one certain place on the log. This site, often no more than eight inches wide, is called the "drumming stage." The log that is used most often is his "primary" log, and the other logs that may be used from time to time are referred to as being his "alternate" logs. But the logs that are used by one male may not be used by another, so there are further classifications based on how additional grouse use a certain site.

The logs and centers used by a sequence of drummers are called "perennial" logs and centers. The real test of the perennial nature of a site is to have it vacant for at least one season, so that a new occupant -- having no knowledge of prior drumming activity -- would be selecting the site purely on the basis of its ecological attributes. Some other centers are considered to be perennial after five or six different birds use the site without interruption. On the Cloquet Forest, there are 88 centers that have been used by five or more drummers, and 27 by 10 or more. It is seldom, however, that all of these centers are occupied in any one year.

One other group that are also considered to be perennial activity centers are those that are not used consecutively, but may be used for two or three years by two or three birds, be vacant for five or six years, and then be used again for several years by a succession of birds. These centers are most likely to be used during periods of population highs. But when a grouse population slump occurs, those are the first perennial centers to beome vacant and remain so until the population starts to recover.

By contrast, we have other activity centers at Cloquet that have been occupied on almost an annual basis regardless of whether the population was high or low. If grouse are any place in the forest, they'll be using those centers.

Another category of use occurs when an activity center proves attractive enough to have perennial use, but none of the logs have top quality cover around them. In this case, each bird occupying that center will probably select a different log than was used by his predecessors. These we consider to be transient logs in a perennial center. Some perennial centers at Cloquet contain as many as 17 transient logs.

Many other logs and activity centers are used by one male grouse as long as he survives, but once he's gone, the log and site become vacant. Those we call "transient" logs and centers. Most transient logs are not used by a second grouse, but a few may be used by a single bird for one or two seasons and then be vacant 10 to 12 years before being used again.

While the characteristics of the drumming log are important to only the male ruffed grouse, the characteristics of his activity center are important to both sexes. The male spends most of his life in this place, and a female will be here for at least the seven months when habitat resources are most limited. So the attributes of the male's activity center are critical to the survival of a ruffed grouse population.

The drumming sound is made by the bird leaning back on his tail and striking his wings against the air violently enough to create a momentary vacuum, much as lightning does when it flashes through the sky. A typical drum consists of a flurry of rapid wing beats lasting five to eight seconds. Contrary to some of the tales one hears, the male grouse does not beat on a log with his wings, nor does he peck the log to drum.

The intervals between drums are generally about four minutes, but if a male is excited by the presence of a hen nearby, his drums may come one minute apart. At other times, when a single bird is drumming and not being answered by others, the intervals between drums may be at multiples of four minutes, that is, at eight, 12, or 16-minute intervals. This occurs most often in late spring, through the summer, and into the fall.

A study by Dr. Herbert Archibald using miniature radio transmitters attached to grouse has provided some information about the timing of drumming. Using a remote radio-tracking system on the Cedar Creek Area in central Minnesota, Archibald found that many drummers moved onto their logs in the middle of the night. Much drumming was done in the early morning hours, long before sunrise [2]. Archibald's study showed some differences between drummers, but generally the intervals between drums were longest at night, varying from four to six minutes, and shortest about sunrise, with three to four minute intervals. During each session of drumming, the intervals between drums became longer and longer and drumming eventually stopped. Evidently, the birds finally got tired and stopped to rest. After a period of inactivity, they repeated the sequence again.

Drumming is strenuous exercise. The energy used to drum, plus the extended periods the birds spend on their logs during the peak of the spring

To produce the drumming sound, the cock leans back on his spread tail and strikes his wings against the air in a flurry that creates a momentary vacuum.

season, causes them to sustain significant weight losses. Based on recaptures of males during the drumming season, it appears that active drummers lose about one-half percent of their weight daily during the three weeks of most intensive activity. Thus a male that weighs 21 oz. in mid-April may be as light as 19 oz. by mid-May.

After the diminishing of drumming activity in early May, males begin to regain weight and are usually back to their mid-April weight by early June.

Drumming can be heard quite a distance under the right conditions. Birds along a lakeshore may be heard a half-mile or farther across a lake. In wooded areas, drumming is seldom heard more than a quarter of a mile and often no farther than an eighth of a mile, particularly in areas of heavy spruce or fir cover which muffles the sound.

People often report a ventriloquistic quality to drumming, and sometimes this seems to be true. But during the quarter of a century that I've been working with drumming grouse, there has seldom been a time that I haven't been able to find the bird, or at least the log he was using, after four or five drums.

Occasionally, though, drummers will prove difficult to find and a certain bird will sound as if it is either ventriloquist or two different grouse. Some grouse alternate position on the log, facing one direction for one drum, then turning for the next drum. This usually makes it sound as if the bird is drumming in different locations. There may be as much as 30 to 40 degrees difference between the apparent direction of a drum when a bird is facing one way and then another.

During the peak of drumming activity, some really "fired-up" drummers will leave their logs upon the approach of an observer and circle through the surrounding woods. These birds move from log to log, still maintaining the four-minute drumming interval. On several occasions, I've had drumming males lead me over as much as 10 acres during a half-hour chase, eventually returning to the logs where they were originally drumming. This behavior can be quite confusing to someone trying to find a drummer,

and is probably one basis for the apparent ventriloquistic characteristic of drumming.

Some male ruffed grouse may not be successful at drumming when they first occupy drumming logs. In the spring of 1961, one male at Cloquet used a log all season and was never heard drumming. Several times we watched him go through all the proper motions, but he was unable to make the drumming sound. All that could be heard when he drummed was the sound of air rushing through his wings. By the following fall he had learned to drum properly, but after doing so, was bagged by a hunter during a special research hunt held on the Cloquet Forest that fall.

Drummers can also vary the intensity of the drumming sound. On occasion, a bird within sight has drummed so faintly that it sounded as though it was hundreds of feet distant. When an observer is that close to a drumming grouse, the rush of air going through the bird's wings is often more noticeable than the drum.

From time to time, we hear reports of "tame" ruffed grouse. These are birds that respond to the activities of people in a manner somewhat contradictory to their normal shyness. While whoever reports these incidents seldom determines the sex of the bird, I suspect they are always males, and most frequently adult males.

Drumming is a stimulus among male grouse.
A classic "drumming duel" occurs when two
or more males respond to one another with
intense, prolonged flurries.

Not all males are initially successful at drumming. We observed one male at Cloquet which made the proper motions all season but never produced a single drumming sound!

WEATHER CONDITIONS AND DRUMMER ACTIVITY

Various factors can affect the likelihood of hearing drumming at a particular time or during a particular day. Obviously, drumming is most likely to be heard during peak season, but even then local conditions affect drumming activity.

Temperature plays a role. During late April in northern Minnesota, the highest level of activity is usually when sunrise temperatures are between 26 and 36° F and rising rapidly. If the early morning temperature is above 42° F, few male grouse will be drumming.

During the week-long drumming peak, a light rain or drizzle does not discourage drumming, but a heavy rainshower or snowstorm turns the birds off. Windy conditions don't discourage drumming, but make it difficult to hear and locate drummers. A still, foggy morning seems to be a particularly satisfactory time for drumming, and most males associated with logs will be active. Fog seems to create a resonance or has capacity to transmit sound which amplifies and increases the loudness of drumming.

The "tame" grouse are not really tame at all. They really are males so aggressive in the defense of their territories that they lose their normal fear of humans. I am familiar with the stories of three such birds, and they were all males. One that lived on the Cloquet Forest in 1956 and 1957 was so aggressive that it would intercept Bob Eng when he walked through this bird's territory. It also used to respond to the radios in parked cars occupied by Cloquet teen-agers, and to a group of forestry students listening for displaying woodcock.

These males were not "tame" in any sense of the word, nor were they fearless. While they might attack a person from behind, they'd back away when faced. They would step onto an opened hand and allow themselves to be lifted above the ground, but they would not allow another hand to be brought close to them; they would not tolerate being restrained in any manner. These males were "tame" only as long as they were in a free and dominant role.

The drumming behavior of the male ruffed grouse is used by wildlife managers to keep track of the changes in grouse numbers [56]. In several states, this is the primary means used to determine year-to-year population trends. Wildlife managers making roadside drumming counts travel selected routes, beginning about a half-hour before sunrise and stopping at predetermined intervals, usually about a mile apart. There they listen for four minutes and record the numbers of drums heard. Usually these routes include about 10 to 12 stops and span the early-morning period of most intensive drumming activity.

While drumming counts are a poor estimate of grouse numbers, the amount of drumming heard each spring provides a fairly accurate forecast of how many grouse will be harvested by hunters the following fall.

This contradictory statement results from the variation in behavior related to bird vigor. Following unfavorable winters, there may not be as much drive to engage in reproductive activity as there is following more favorable winters. This will be discussed in detail later, but for now, let's say that there are seasons when drumming activity is greatly reduced, and perhaps only one-quarter to one-half of the males occupying drumming logs are likely to be heard on a certain day. This depression in drumming activity is also expressed by markedly decreased log attendance and, most importantly, by a reduction in reproductive effort, nesting, and chick production.

In other breeding seasons, when winter conditions have been more favorable, there may be half as many males on logs, but the drumming counts will be higher because the birds are really excited about the approaching breeding season, and most, if not all, will be heard drumming each morning. This arouses the hens too, so there is a maximum reproductive effort resulting in many young grouse wandering around the woods in the fall.

As the tempo of drumming increases during the spring, the percentage of birds engaging in drumming each morning gradually increases. Finally, at the peak of drumming during good years, as many as 85 to 90 percent of the drummers may be active any given morning. But this peak only lasts about five days. Around Lake Superior, the peak of drumming usually occurs between the 25th and 29th of April, but may be three or four days earlier or later, depending upon the season. By the 5th of May, only a small portion of birds are still actively drumming on a daily basis. This is followed by a period of about 10 days when very little drumming is heard, then about the 15th of May drumming activity increases again, with drumming most often heard in the evening into early June.

Drummers show so little interest in attending their logs and drumming in early May that at Cloquet we routinely close down the mirror trapping operations from about May 5th to the 15th.

Farther south in Minnesota, the peak of drumming is about a week earlier [2,55]. In northeastern Iowa, the peak of drumming is about April 8 to 14 [52], and in northern Georgia, drumming extends from late March to mid-May [34]. In western Washington, at about the same latitude as Minnesota's North Shore, the peak of drumming occurs between March 26 and April 7 [9].

Most of the male grouse engaging in drumming activity early in the spring were established on their logs the previous fall, if not earlier. These are the grouse that contribute to the late-April peak in activity and whose drumming tapers off markedly in early May. They probably do most of the breeding.

Another group of drummers enters the picture in early May. These are smaller males that failed to find suitable logs the previous fall and aren't settled until the established drummers have largely completed their season. Some of these are two-year-old birds that may even be smaller than most hens and were unable to compete during the earlier part of the breeding season. These birds never reach the intensity of drumming evident earlier, but they do engage in quite a bit of drumming later in May. This late-season drumming tends to be rather sporadic and is as likely to occur late in the afternoon and after sunset as in the morning.

The phases of the moon have some bearing on drumming activity. When a full moon coincides with the peak of drumming, night use of logs is more common than when the moon is not so bright. On several occasions when the moon was full, using a headlamp, I have sneaked close enough to touch drummers on their logs.

In seasons when ruffed grouse are particularly numerous, there may not be enough acceptable drumming sites for all the birds that would like to drum [27]. Under these conditions, some birds exist as virtual phantoms in the grouse population and are not counted by our conventional inventory techniques. From time to time, when the established drummer in an activity center is busily drumming elsewhere, some of these birds will drum. If the dominant bird in the activity center quits drumming during one of these drumming duels, the subordinate male usually ceases drumming as well. Apparently, as long as the subordinate bird knows that the dominant male is on his log drumming, he feels fairly secure drumming nearby. When he doesn't hear the dominant male drumming, he probably believes it is appropriate to be quiet and moves off the log to avoid being challenged.

Some activity centers traditionally have two males present. One is clearly the dominant bird and he does most if not all of the drumming. He is also the bird that we usually trap and band. But the other male will be seen in the center, usually not too close to the dominant male. These centers with two males often have rapid turnover so that each spring a new, unbanded male is the dominant bird. Repeatedly these unbanded, replacement males have been identified as adults, that is, at least 22 or 23 months-old, and of the same color-phase as the unbanded, non-drummer we saw in that center a year earlier.

Being big has value to a male ruffed grouse. Once a bird has been able to establish himself in a drumming activity center, the larger he is, the better success he will have in defending his center against intrusion by other males. This is reflected in the heavier weights of males that remain on the same log throughout their lives or shift to other logs within the same activity center. Although the differences are not great, males shifting from one activity center to another have generally been lighter in weight than those remaining on one log for their lifetimes.

Birds moving onto "new" logs for the first time tend to be young males in their first season and heavier than males who replace other males on perennial logs.

The "might makes right" effect has other implications for the population. Sometimes the grouse of one year's hatch, or "cohort," are smaller than normal. This usually occurs when the population is declining. With lessened competition, these smaller males have little problem finding vacant drumming logs and may occupy some quite choice sites. But if the next year's cohort of young grouse is normal-sized, or larger than normal, displacement of established, smaller, older drummers occurs when these young males begin occupying logs. Then the smaller, older males are forced to shift to another activity center which almost always is in markedly poorer habitat than the ones from which they

When a goshawk passes through the area, most, if not all of the drummers fall discreetly silent. The sudden silence of one bird seems to serve as a warning for all.

were displaced.

On occasion, though, two evenly-matched male ruffed grouse may occupy drumming sites quite close together in the spring. At Cloquet, we've had drummers occupying, for most of a season, sites within 100 feet of each other. In every instance, these have been situations where a large, young male was successful in challenging and sharing a single activity center with an older male. When both birds have been trapped and handled, we found they were virtually identical in weight and size.

Being big has its advantages, but it also has disadvantages. The largest grouse have the best likelihood of occupying the best-quality sites. By occupying a perennial center, the big bird is more likely to engage in breeding activity and pass his genes onto the next generation. But by occupying that center, he also is less likely to live to a second year. The life span of replacement birds in perennial activity centers tends to be shorter than for the first birds occupying transient logs in transient centers. Or, for that matter, even transient logs in perennial centers [32]. The bird in a new activity center may not have as much opportunity for breeding, but he's more likely to live to a second breeding season.

These persistently-used perennial centers are not only "ecological magnets," but often they also prove to be "ecological traps." It appears that the long-lived raptors become familiar with the deficiencies in cover around perennial centers. While they are seldom successful in taking the occupant off his log, they apparently learn that if they perch in certain places often enough, at some time during the season the resident drummer will expose himself in a vulnerable situation. A study of the sites where predation occurred at Cloquet showed that cover at kill sites was significantly poorer than around drumming logs [69].

When hens are entering their estrous cycle, they may be hurriedly seeking a male to mate with. Then the big male occupying a log or center with a history of perennial use has the advantage. Female grouse are likely to visit a perennial log whether or not a drummer is present. They'll mate if a male is present, otherwise

they'll move on seeking another male, and may even be attracted by drumming in a transient site [5].

Summer and fall drumming is purely territorial in function. Many established drummers return to their logs periodically throughout the summer and are heard drumming from time to time, usually on a warm afternoon.

Our visits to drumming logs through the summer show the frequency at which many birds return. It is not uncommon to find molted primary feathers which are shed by males while engaging in drumming activity. Since these feathers are shed at approximately one-week intervals, they provide additional evidence of the continued summer use of logs by the birds [76].

The intensity of fall drumming is largely a response to pressure from young males dispersing from their brood range. Fall drumming by established males usually reaches its peak in early or mid-October. This coincides with the period when young males are most actively searching for areas where they will spend the rest of their lives. Drumming by newly-established young males begins in late October and steadily increases as their claim to an activity center or territory is strengthened.

Although I've talked of the "drumming log," grouse do not need a hollow log to drum on nor do they need a big, old, moss-covered log for their display platform. As a matter of fact, they don't need a log at all. A male ruffed grouse will readily use as drumming sites such diverse objects as boulders, mounds of dirt, wood piles, roots of trees, road culverts, and even the snowbanks along roadways. Drumming grouse frequently use rock walls as drumming sites in New England where old pastures have reverted to forests.

Although the sites they may find acceptable for drumming are quite diverse, the nature of all those sites have certain common traits which make them attractive. Inexperienced young males may select almost any sort of a situation which provides them with an apparently adequate drumming facility. But when one examines the types of sites used repeatedly by a succession of drummers over a number of years, we find that there are some fairly precise qualities to the sites. Also, the longevity of the grouse using these sites has to be taken into consideration when judging their worth.

Whey they have a choice, that is, when there is a range of sites available to them, the male grouse prefers to use a log or a site that places him nine to 15 inches above the ground on a log that is usually 20 to 40 feet long. The bird choosing a drumming log has two primary considerations. One is to select a site that gives him the maximum opportunity to advertise his presence; second, to select a site which gives him maximum security.

Drumming male grouse are not particularly choosy about the condition of the log they use so long as it meets their primary requirements as a drumming stage. They commonly use the traditional moss-covered log and may continue to use it until it has rotted down to a mound of wood dust. But they will also use freshly-fallen logs. On one occasion, a male was using a 10-foot red pine bolt that had been cut in the winter. The bird continued using this log right up to when it was taken to a sawmill. In other instances, we have felled trees to be drumming logs. When those logs were felled in the proper habitats, they were accepted and some have been used by drummers for a number of years. A spruce log felled in 1972 in good cover has been a primary log for a decade.

Perennial drumming sites are invariably in situations where the bird has the best opportunities to see his surroundings. Out of a sample of 465 logs that have been used as primary logs at Cloquet for the past 27 years, 70.5 percent had no objects within a 50 to 60-foot radius that would provide concealment for a fox, bobcat, or other four-footed predator.

When choosing drumming sites, ruffed grouse males are partial to uprooted trees having a large root mass at one end. On this sort of site, the birds will usually select a drumming stage on the trunk about three to five feet from the root mass which serves as a "guard object." A root mass provides protection against predation for as

much as an eighth to a quarter of the horizon. Where there is no root mass, the drumming site will be about 18 inches from a tree trunk, a clump of shrubs, or a stump or snag. This guard object gives them additional protection. Guard objects have been present at 378 of 432 (87.5%) logs used as primary sites on the Cloquet Forest.

The drumming site will usually be on a log which is surrounded by moderately dense hardwood regeneration or brush. This should extend at least three feet above the level of the log and more often 15 to 20 feet. At preferred sites, the density of hardwood saplings is usually in the range of 3,000 to 7,000 stems per acre. If the surrounding vegetation consists of smaller brush stems, the densities are more likely to range from 3,000 to 9,700 per acre. This vertical cover should have a fairly even distribution around the drumming stage to provide optimal protection for the drumming male. The drumming male also needs a clear escape route from the log, a path where there are few branches or stems to impede rapid movement by a fleeing bird.

Good drumming sites are quite predator-proof. The Cloquet Project provides evidence of this. We've dealt with drumming male grouse for over a quarter of a century and have records on the use of over 2,000 logs by over 1,350 birds. During that period, we have recorded only 19 instances of drummers being taken by predators at or close to drumming logs. In spite of the drumming and the amount of time that a male grouse may spend on his log, he is probably more secure there than at any other time in his life. We have never seen evidence of predation at a log that was in really good cover.

The male grouse selecting a drumming log considers other aspects of the site as well. For example, if the bird is selecting a log in a site where several logs are down, the chosen log is invariably higher than the other logs. Also, if the log is on level ground, the selected log will normally place the bird somewhat higher off the ground than if the log is either at the foot of the slope or on the break of a slope. Topography gives the bird an advantage in these latter situations, and a smaller-diameter log may be selected than would be chosen on a level site.

One other characteristic that seems to be important to ruffed grouse choosing drumming logs in northern Minnesota is the proximity of mature, male aspens in the forest canopy. Among 727 primary drumming logs in perennial centers, 82 percent either had aspen overhead or within sight of the log. Only eight percent of the repeatedly-used drumming sites have been more than 100 yards from aspen. Of 342 transient logs that have been occupied by only one drummer during the past quarter century, 16 percent were farther than 100 yards from aspen. This could have been one reason why they were transient sites. A few of these transient sites were used by one drummer for as long as five years.

Good logs in proper situations will be used for long periods of time. There are at least three logs on the Cloquet Forest with histories of use from 1932 or 1933, and several other logs have had nearly continuous use since the current project started in 1956. There are several logs on the Cloquet Forest in use in the late 1950's and early 1960's where the forest was later clear-cut. After a decade, the cover regenerated and those logs have come back into use. Some have been in use for over a decade and are now in deteriorating coverts that are losing their value for ruffed grouse.

Decay also determines how long logs will last. Big old pine, spruce, oak, or maple logs last for many years. Balsam fir logs seldom last more than 10 years, and aspen logs also break down within a few years. The outer bark of paper birch is durable enough to provide a drumming site even when the interior wood has crumbled. There are some piles of birch logs on the Cloquet Forest, cut for firewood by the CCC in the 1930's and left in the woods, which have been used for drumming within the last 20 years.

Old rock walls and the scattered boulders left by glaciers last, of course, practically forever. Their use is determined more by the quality of cover around the site than by the durability of the object.

Most male grouse continue to use their logs as long as they live. Evidence of use is provided by

Ruffed grouse do not exclusively require logs for drumming sites. Such diverse objects as boulders, dirt mounds, wood piles, and even roadway snowbanks are used by males.

various signs. The most common evidence is an accumulation of fecal droppings, but feathers molted through the summer, drumming activity in spring and fall, leaves blown away by drumming, and fresh tracks in the snow through the winter also show that a bird is still there. If any of these signs ceases abruptly, it usually signals the death of the occupant.

A change of occupants can occur almost unnoticed. Sometimes another, previously-inactive, male grouse shares the area with the more active bird and will replace him within a matter of hours or a few days. On an early morning in April, 1959, a forestry student located a new log on the Cloquet Forest. He showed me the log at noon, but by then a raptor had found the bird too, and only feathers were left of the occupant. That evening, a trap was placed on the log anyway, and another grouse was captured the next morning.

Frequently, when a grouse has been "fighting" the trap after capture and has injured himself, the trap is left set on the log and another male captured there a day or two later.

The fidelity exhibited by a male grouse to a log or certain logs seems to be largely a measure of quality of the habitat at the specific site. A grouse that has selected a log providing adequate security is likely to use only one log as his primary log and seldom moves to another log.

If the quality of the habitat is not so good and a bird is uneasy about using one log all the time, he may use two or three different logs about equally. On the other hand, if the best log has markedly

When choosing drumming sites, male grouse are partial to uprooted trees with exposed root masses that serve as "guard objects."

better habitat than any others nearby but still is not really secure, a bird may use that log as his primary site and use two or three other logs as alternate sites for occasional drumming.

While male ruffed grouse that have chosen secure sites for drumming continue to use those sites as long as they live, males that initially select poorer sites often move to better sites before the next drumming season. At Cloquet, about 25 percent of the males surviving from their first spring to the next fall will have shifted to different drumming logs over the summer. These shifts have nearly always been from a poorer to a better site, and from transient logs or centers to perennial logs and centers.

Forest habitats occupied by ruffed grouse are dynamic, living systems, subject to change over a period of years. Sometimes we forget that when we look at shrubs and trees, and nothing much seems to change over a period of two or three

years. But when careful measurements are taken, and the development of a forest is watched for a quarter of a century (or even a decade in some instances), changes that are hardly perceptible in two or three years become obvious.

Grouse are sensitive to these changes. It is not so much a matter of the individual bird responding to gradual changes, but of the succession of birds that check that habitat each fall. They must have a feeling about what is a comfortable and secure place to occupy.

This changed feeling about a certain covert is most often expressed in rather subtle ways. A drumming log that has been used as the primary site by a succession of males for a number of years begins being used as an alternate log by a replacement bird. Or maybe it is only that after years of exclusive use of one log in a center, a replacement begins using two or three other logs as well. The occupants are likely to become harder to approach and more difficult to trap. Then in one or two years, the center is abandoned. When we re-examine the site critically, we see that significant changes have occurred in the nature of the vegetation around the log.

The best habitats for ruffed grouse are satisfactory for the shortest period of time. The sapling aspen stands that support the highest densities of wintering and breeding grouse begin providing acceptable cover when they are five to 10 years-old (the exact timing depends upon local growing conditions) and have "gone-by" at 15 to 25 years of age.

Poorer-quality coverts in older, more static forest sites may be used for a longer period of time, but the breeding grouse density will probably always be one-quarter or less that common to the rapidly-developing, younger forest.

We have one perennial activity center on the Cloquet Forest that has always been quite attractive for grouse but is a rather high risk area. It

has a good distribution of dense hazel cover and many fine logs. There is an abundance of male aspens in the forest canopy. From 1956 to 1983, this center has been used for 17 years by 14 drumming males which indicates just how perennial this area has been. For that matter, the history of grouse use in this center began in 1933. However, the center is surrounded by a coniferous forest, primarily jack pine, but with balsam fir, spruce, and red pine also in the forest stand. As might be expected, this coniferous canopy has provided fine cover for raptors. As a consequence, turnover there has been fairly rapid. Only three drummers that have occupied this center have survived from one drumming season to a second, and none have survived to a third season. There's an unusual aspect in the history of this center: Three different birds which evidently recognized the hazard of living there moved elsewhere after their first spring. One of the males moved northwest 3,600 feet where he

Good drumming sites are quite predator proof. In spite of the time and activity spent on the log, a male grouse is probably more secure there than at any other period.

survived for at least another six months, and the other two moved to the southeast. One of the latter was recaptured 3,600 feet from the abandoned activity center in summer trapping but was never found on a drumming log, and the other bird was retaken on a drumming log 3,360 feet from this center a year later.

The drumming season is a period of increased hazard for ruffed grouse, especially those birds associated with drumming logs. During the two or three-week period of most intensive drumming, most of the drummers spend most of their time on a log. Although they have usually selected a situation that provides optimum protection from a surprise attack, they still are exposed to increased risk. By drumming, they are attracting attention to themselves, and this is an invitation for predators to lurk nearby. They can wait for the bird to leave the security of the drumming site and move into a situation where he is vulnerable. Logs in activity centers having few such "ecological traps" tend to be used by longer-lived grouse, but many activity centers that provide security for the drummer may provide relatively little protection when he moves away from the log.

Chapter Four

NESTING

After mating, the hen may leave the activity center of her mate and never see that male again, for he takes no part in the nesting activity nor in brood rearing.

The mated hen searches for a suitable site for her nest. The site selected may be within a few hundred feet of the log of the male with whom she mated, or she may move a half-mile, passing through the activity centers of one or two other males, and possibly nesting not far from the drumming log of still another male with whom she has no apparent contact [5].

The nest is a bowl formed in the leaves on the forest floor. It is usually at the base of some upright object which provides protection from one side. This object may be a tree, stump, boulder, or a large log. Occasionally, a hen will place her nest in a brush pile or under a log. We have even seen nests out in the open, several yards from any protection. The hen selects a site where she has unrestricted vision of the surrounding forest floor for a distance of 50 to 60 feet. She probably consciously selects a situation where a cat or fox would have difficulty getting within pouncing distance of her without being seen. Also, here in northern Minnesota, hens almost invariably nest close to a clone of male aspens. If they're not nesting at the base of one of these trees, then they're almost surely within sight of them.

Studies of feeding behavior made by John Kupa, and later by Philip Schladweiler, showed that much of the feeding activity during incubation involved hens flying from near the nest, up into the aspens overhead, and feeding on the leaves. [44,66] A hen grouse was never observed feeding on the leaves of a female aspen at Cloquet, but Stephen Maxson recorded nesting hens feeding on the leaves of female aspen in a later study in east-central Minnesota [51].

By walking only a short distance from the nest before flying into the aspens overhead, or nearby, and then flying back close to the nest before resuming incubation, the hen avoids leaving a scent trail that keen-nosed mammals could follow to find her nest.

The typical nest is in a fairly open situation on the ground. Rather than seeking a place where she is hidden, the female grouse prefers to depend upon cryptic coloration which makes her virtually invisible to animals that may be hunting for her. She prefers an open site where she has fairly unrestricted surveillance for some distance around her nest site. This allows her to detect the approach of any predators that might pose a threat. It allows the hen the option of either

*The nest is a bowl formed in the leaves
of the forest floor. On the North Shore,
hens almost invariably nest close
to a clone of male aspens.*

Most nests are found at the base of an upright object, be it tree, stump, boulder, or log that offers protection from one side and unrestricted vision from the other.

Rather than seeking a nest-site where she's hidden, the hen depends upon cryptic coloration to hide her from the searching eyes of predators.

sneaking off the nest before she is seen or sitting tight and depending upon her cryptic coloration to keep her from being spotted. As long as she can watch a predator in the vicinity of her nest, she retains the option of judging whether or not she is in imminent danger -- there is no point in her needlessly leaving her nest if she can safely remain on it. A nest covered by a grouse is very difficult to see, but an uncovered clutch of eggs is conspicuous from some distance. If her life is threatened, the obvious choice is to flee, even if she gives away the location of her nest and sacrifices the eggs by doing so; as long as the hen is alive, she can renest.

Many ruffed grouse hens are so confident in their ability to remain unseen on the nest that they will permit close approach. Several times I've touched nesting hens before they'd leave the nest.

During a search for nests with a group of eight forestry students, we found one especially tenacious hen. We were taking a break in our search and were mostly sitting around in a group talking. After we'd been there for several minutes, one of the crew, leaning against an aspen, looked down and saw a hen sitting tight on her nest less than two feet from his feet. She stayed in place as we moved away, leaving her undisturbed.

There is no attempt to line the nest, though during incubation feathers may accumulate in the nest as a result of the hen preening herself. Egg laying commences about three to five days

after mating, and they are laid at intervals of a day to a day and a half apart, or at about 24 to 30-hour intervals. It may take about 15 days for a ruffed grouse hen to lay the average clutch of 10 eggs, or as long as 20 days to lay a 14-egg clutch.

The ruffed grouse hen makes no effort to incubate her eggs until the clutch is complete. During the laying period, she is at the nest only long enough to lay the eggs and then leaves it's vicinity. Radio-tracking has shown that the hen is at the nest for an hour or longer to lay an egg so.

Once I came upon a hen that was preparing to lay her first egg in a new nest. She had shaped a neat nest-bowl on the south side of a tree trunk, but had not laid the first egg. When she ran off, she had a decided droop in her rear end. Several days later, there were 10 eggs in the nest, but she was nesting too near a well-used game trail and the nest was destroyed shortly afterwards.

From the time it takes to lay the eggs and then incubate them for more than three weeks, a ruffed grouse hen spends about five weeks in association with the nest-site. This prolonged attachment to a specific place makes it especially important that the female chooses a situation which provides maximum security for her and her eggs.

Hens generally remain on the nest throughout the night, but may leave the nest two to four times during the day. Most often, hens are off the nest early in the morning and late in the afternoon, but they may also leave occasionally at other times during the day. The duration of these breaks in incubation ranges from about 15 to 40

Of this large, 14-egg clutch, it is likely that one or two chicks will perish because they failed to hatch in time to leave with the rest of the brood.

minutes, and totals from a half-hour to an hour and a half daily 44,50. Usually the hen only leaves the nest to feed, and she doesn't cover the eggs when she leaves. Incubation lasts approximately 23 to 24 days before the first eggs are pipped. Once pipping begins, it takes from 8 to 36 hours for the eggs to hatch 18. "Pipping" refers to the activity of the chick in the egg, when it breaks the eggshell from the inside. Grouse chicks have a special "egg tooth" on their bills for this particular and important event. The egg tooth soon disappears as the chick begins to grow.

An interesting sidelight to the incubation and hatching of chicks involves communication between chicks while still in the eggs, and between the incubating hen and her developing chicks. While this story has not been documented for ruffed grouse, we know it occurs among both bobwhite quail and wood ducks 21. This happens in ruffed grouse nests and among many other birds with large clutches laid over a period of two or three weeks that need to have all the chicks hatching nearly simultaneously.

What has been learned in these other species is that the incubating hen makes evenly-spaced clucking sounds during the late stages of incubation. These sounds serve to imprint the chicks to her voice. At the same time, the chicks in the eggs are communicating with one another 23,75. This brings all the chicks into synchronous development and assures that even though the eggs were laid over a period of two or three weeks, they will all hatch within a few hours of one

Inside their eggs the chicks use the temporary "egg-tooth" on their bills to pip the shell. Once pipping begins, it takes about 24 hours for the eggs to hatch.

another.

Once the majority of the eggs hatch and the chicks have dried off and are becoming active, the hen crosses a hormonal threshold, changing her behavior from that of an incubating bird to a brooding hen. In this latter mode, she is ready to lead her brood from the nest to a brood range where they will spend the rest of the summer.

Usually all of the eggs hatch in clutches which number no more than 10 to 12 eggs. But when there are 14 or more eggs in a clutch, it is common to find one or two chicks that perished because they did not hatch soon enough to leave the nest with the rest of the brood.

A fairly high percentage of the nests are lost to predation each year. At Cloquet over the years, about 32 percent of the nests we knew about were destroyed before they hatched. In the classic New York study, Dr. Gardiner Bump and his co-workers recorded destruction of nearly 39 percent of the nests 12.

Several animals may be regarded as potential threats to a clutch of unattended eggs. Crows and jays, and gray, fox, and red squirrels, and woodchucks are all common animals in coverts where ruffed grouse nest, and all will eat eggs if they can find them. Even chipmunks have been known to roll eggs from grouse nests while the hen was absent. Of course, skunks, raccoons, foxes, coyotes, dogs, bobcats, and house cats always pose a threat to both the hen and her eggs.

On the North Shore of Lake Superior, most

Once the majority of the eggs hatch, the hen crosses a hormonal threshold, changing her behavior from that of an incubating bird to that of a brooding hen.

It has been learned that, while still in their eggs, ruffed grouse chicks communicate with the hen and among one another to ensure synchronous hatching of the clutch.

After hatching, the brood remains with the hen for 16 to 18 weeks or, on the North Shore, until about the middle of September.

nests hatch during the first two weeks in June. Farther south, in central Minnesota the peak of hatching is during the last week of May and the first week of June, which is the same timing as in central Wisconsin and in New York [12,43].

The size of young grouse varies from year to year. All the grouse hatched in one year (a cohort), may weigh significantly less than the young birds produced in another year. These variations in weight seem to be related to the severity of winter stress endured by breeding hens prior to egg laying. As discussed later in the chapter on winter, this stress may be caused by insufficient food resources, improper snow conditions, unsatisfactory temperature conditions, or a combination of all. Young grouse that are small in the fall, and presumably were smaller than normal when they hatched, never make up that deficiency. The consequences for a male being smaller than average have already been discussed in the chapter on drumming. We don't know what the disadvantages may be for a hen smaller than normal, but suspect that a small hen may produce a brood of chicks less vigorous than those produced by a larger hen.

Occasionally, we hear about second broods of ruffed grouse. But this seems to be a very unlikely event. The evidence we have is that broods that show up later in the season are most likely to be the final successful nesting of a hen who has lost one or more clutches earlier. After hatching, the brood and the hen tend to remain together until the chicks are 16 to 18-weeks old, which is about the middle of September.

On September 20, 1982, a hunter found a living day-old chick and brought it to me. If there ever was evidence of a second brood, that would have been it because that chick's egg would have been laid in the middle of August. But I suspect that this hen had lost earlier clutches, or perhaps an earlier brood, and finally nested successfully.

There is little advantage in renesting and producing a second brood. If the chicks have not hatched by the middle of June, they will not be fully grown by fall and are less likely to survive the winter.

One of the factors that seems to be crucial to increasing grouse populations is a nearly simultaneous hatch. A hatch spread over several weeks is most likely to result in either a static population or a decline in numbers the following years.

Chapter Five

SUMMER

Summer is a season for growth and renewal. It is the season when plant cover provides the greatest security for grouse, and there is an abundance of food. Ruffed grouse are literally surrounded by things they can eat in the summer. In the next chapter, we describe the summer-long growth of young ruffed grouse as they change from small chicks to full-size grouse in about 16 weeks. For adults, it is a period of recovery from the rigors of winter and the breeding season. It is the season of plumage renewal.

A succession of fruits is produced through the summer, and most forest sites occupied by ruffed grouse have an abundance of these. Prominent among the early summer fruits are the strawberries, raspberries, pin- and chokecherries, and juneberries. Grouse habitat is usually teeming with many insects, caterpillars, and worms of one sort or another, food for both young and adult grouse, and the green, developing seeds of some of the grasses and the sedges become available. There is an abundance of succulent leaves of many herbaceous plants the birds desire. The tough, fleshy leaves of the aspen are a particularly important summer food resource for adult grouse [23]. This is the season of abundance.

The ready availability of food and the protec-tion of heavy cover makes summer the logical time for ruffed grouse to replace their worn plumage and to regain the weight they lost during the rigors of breeding and nesting.

Ruffed grouse do not seem to need drinking water *per se* during the summer. Most of the food they take in the summer has a very high water content and that alone appears to meet their needs. Many grouse spend the summer in places where water is readily available to them, but this preference is probably due to the nature of the vegetation in the wetter sites rather than the presence of water. In the Lakes States many ruffed grouse, both adults and broods, spend much of the summer among the alders in wet, lowland swales or along streams. While this might indicate a summertime need for drinking water, I believe it more often means that this is the most secure and lush habitat available, and grouse are there for that reason. Certainly, on the Cloquet Forest and on the North Shore, the alder bottoms are infinitely better summer places for ruffed grouse than the dry, upland pine stands that often border them.

Where aspen sapling stands have developed on drier, upland sites, ruffed grouse usually abandon the alder lowlands, showing a marked preference for the coolness and abundant food

*During summer, ruffed grouse cleanse their
plumage and discourage parasites by
"dusting". Dusting sites include anthills,
sand, and the dirt among uprooted trees.*

resources in the young aspen.

Ruffed grouse cleanse their plumage and discourage external parasites by dusting. The dirt of ant hills is often chosen for dusting, as are crumbled logs or stumps and the dirt among the roots of uprooted trees. It is common to find evidence of much dusting among the roots of wind-thrown trees that are also being used as drumming logs.

The males begin molting in early June, losing the first four primary flight feathers by the end of the month. The remaining six primaries are lost and replaced through the summer at intervals of about a week 76. Ruffed grouse are never flightless like waterfowl, although in mid-summer they have lost enough feathers for flight to become labored and difficult. They also replace all of their body feathers during the summer. The tail feathers are lost pretty much at one time in late August after the flight feathers have been replaced.

Many of the adult males continue to use their logs through the summer. We often find a nearly-complete set of the molted primaries lying alongside the log where they fell during the vigorous wing-beating of the drumming bird.

Drumming tends to be rather sporadic during the summer. On warm summer days, it is not uncommon to hear a bird drumming, but it is usually at widely-spaced intervals and not as regular as during the spring and fall.

This is the busy season for hens rearing their

young. The molt of adult hens with broods tends to be delayed, with many adult hens still molting in the early part of the hunting season in September and October. This is long after adult males and non-breeding hens have completed their feather replacement.

Young grouse increase in size quite dramatically, and to keep their body covered with the feather insulation, there is a rapid replacement and growth of feathers. The size feather that will support a 20 to 25 gram week-old chick in flight will hardly support a bird that is about 25 times heavier 15 weeks later. So a replacement, or "post-juvenal molt" of primary feathers commences about the middle of July and continues until the young grouse is 17-weeks old. Then we say that a young ruffed grouse has passed from its "juvenal" to "immature" plumage.

This summer molting provides the means by which the ages of ruffed grouse can be determined, to a certain extent. This technique is based on the progression of molt of the 10 outermost, or primary, feathers on the wing. These are the feathers that are growing from that part of a bird's wing analogous to our hand and fingers. When these feathers are replaced, the molt proceeds from the innermost primary, the first, to the outermost, the tenth. After ruffed grouse are more than a year old and considered adults, this molt is complete. But young grouse, less than four months old in their post-juvenal molt, replace only the first eight primaries. The young

Summer is the season of food abundance for grouse. Most forest sites offer both young and old birds myriad fruits, seeds, succulent leaves, and insects.

grouse's ninth and 10th juvenal primaries are retained until the bird is about 14-months old.

In hunting seasons, if the ninth and 10th primaries are fully grown and seventh or eighth are growing, the bird was hatched that year. If the seventh and eighth are grown or growing, and the ninth and 10th are missing or growing, the bird is more than 14 months old. Once the first adult molt is complete, the age of a ruffed grouse can be determined only if it has been banded as a young bird; there are no other reliable characteristics for determining age. Certainly size has no relationship to the age of a grown ruffed grouse.

When the wing feathers are not in the process of being replaced, the aging technique is based on differences between the juvenal ninth and 10th primaries and the same feathers grown after the bird is over a year old. The difference most commonly recognized is the *pointed* tip of the juvenal 10th primary, as contrasted to a more *rounded* tip on the adult 10th, resembling the tip of the eighth and ninth primaries. A typical juvenal 10th primary has the shape of a paring knife. The tips of the ninth primary on young grouse often shows signs of abrasive wear, or "foxing," resulting from damage incurred while the eighth was being replaced and the ninth was the longest feather on the wing tip. These are relative differences, and one has to examine quite a number of wings to become proficient at determining ages using this technique. Even then,

some birds won't clearly separate into either category.

Usually a more reliable procedure is to examine the bases of the eighth and ninth primaries right where they emerge from the skin. If the tissue-paper-like remnants of the developing feathers "sheathing" is more pronounced on the eighth than on the ninth, the bird is young; if the reverse is true, the bird is older. There are some additional techniques used by biologists which use micrometers to measure feather-shaft diameters. But examining for sheathing is generally adequate, particularly in the fall when most people are handling grouse.

Adult grouse continue to die through the summer, though not as fast as in the spring or fall. At this time of year, mammals are responsible for more predation than raptors. Summer vegetation provides multiple canopies overhead that provide the grouse with good protection from the hawks and owls so long as the grouse stay away from the openings and roadsides or trailsides that provide an opportunity for a perched raptor to swoop upon an unsuspecting, feeding grouse. But during this season, the dense vegetation close to the ground provides an optimal opportunity for mammalian predators to remain concealed where they can take grouse from ambush. This dense summer vegetation, together with the reduced flight capability of grouse that have molted, gives the four-legged predators a better chance to take birds than they have during other seasons.

In the Lakes States, ruffed grouse spend much of their summer among the alders in wet, lush swales or along streams.

Chapter Six

BROOD DEVELOPMENT

Ruffed grouse chicks hatch after about 23 or 24 days of incubation. It takes about 24 hours from the time the eggs start pipping until all the chicks have emerged. The hen continues incubating until most or all of the eggs have hatched and the chicks have dried off. When there are a number of active, peeping chicks under the hen she crosses a threshold in her behavior, changing from an incubating bird to a brooding bird. Then she leads her brood of chicks from the nest, never to return to that site.

The newly-hatched grouse chick is not much larger than a man's thumb and weighs about 12 to 14 grams -- roughly the weight of three nickels. In spite of their small size and seeming helplessness, grouse chicks are quite mobile. After leaving the nest with their mother, they may move as far as three or four miles during the first 10 days -- roughly equivalent to a human walking over 80 miles.

The hen leads her brood in search of an area where they will find a covert that provides security from predation and an abundance of food. The habitat to support rapidly-growing young grouse has to have somewhat different resources than those needed by the nesting hen. In this brood habitat, they will spend the summer and increase their size 40-fold over a 16-week period.

Traditionally, alder lowlands have been considered to be the most important summer habitats for ruffed grouse broods in the Lake States. This is still true in areas where the forests have been undisturbed for a half-century or longer, for there the alder lowlands are the only places with cover dense enough to be brood habitat. This was certainly so when the most intensive brood studies were done on the Cloquet Forest in the early 1960's [5,19,44]. But when grouse hens have a choice of habitats, they clearly prefer upland stands of aspen saplings for their chicks [43]. This is usually five to 15-year-old aspen regeneration, quite open on the forest floor, with a closed canopy 15 to 20 feet overhead. This type of cover provides the least opportunity for predation upon the brood. There is also less danger here of chicks drowning in the wet holes so common in many lowland alder sites.

Chicks begin feeding themselves shortly after they have hatched. For the first day or so, the hen may have to show them what to eat, but even day-old chicks begin eating ants and other small insects. Grouse chicks continue feeding almost exclusively on insects, worms, and other small forms of animal life for the first four or five weeks. Leafhoppers, flies, mosquitos, various bugs, beetles, and ants all come in for attention. Since

Alder lowlands are an important brood habitat. However, a hen prefers upland stands of aspen saplings where her chicks are safer from avian predators and other dangers.

ruffed grouse seldom scratch or turn over leaves looking for food, they feed mostly on things seen on leaves and on the ground. Consuming animal protein is vital in this period of rapid growth. They need protein for feather development, particularly flight feathers.

When the hen herds her brood toward a stand of sapling aspens, she is taking them to the best of all habitats. The abundance of insects will be greater here than in any other part of the forest, including the alder lowlands. Aspen leaf litter is richest in nutrients of any leaf litter in Northern forests. Summer temperatures in these sites tend to be more favorable as well, not cooling off so much at night nor becoming as warm in mid-day as in other forest situations. Even the alder lowlands that have long been considered traditional summer ruffed grouse brood ranges have greater daily temperature fluctuations than occur among the aspen saplings.

Young ruffed grouse chicks can fly by the time they are 10-days old, and they look like large

bumble-bees buzzing through the woods.

When they are about four or five weeks old, young ruffed grouse begin to shift from the diet of animal matter and begin feeding on plant materials. By this time in early July, the developing seeds of the woodland sedges and some of the grasses are in a green, soft-dough stage, and grouse chicks feed heavily on those. Also by mid-summer, strawberries, juneberries, raspberries, pincherries, and a number of other fruits are ripe. From the time they are about a month old, ruffed grouse are primarily herbivores, although they'll still eat insects.

The role the hen plays in taking care of the brood is uncertain. She probably is responsible for showing them what to eat their first two or three days of life, and certainly is a source of protection against wet weather and the cold night air during the early period of chick development. She appears responsible for leading the chicks from the nest to a suitable brood range, and she functions as the lookout for the brood to warn

Although weighing only 12 to 14 grams when newly hatched, young grouse will increase their size some 40-fold over a 16-week period in a suitable covert.

The role the hen plays in caring for the brood is not completely known, but she is certainly an early source of protection against wet weather and the cold night air.

them of impending danger. But once the brood is on its brood range, she no longer seems to be the leader, but rather tags along, keeping the chicks in contact, but allowing them to move ahead of her as they forage for food.

As the chicks grow, it becomes increasingly difficult for the hen to brood them, but as their definitive plumage develops, they become less dependent upon the hen for protection from exposure.

There are few things that occur in the forest in June that can be more startling than the sudden attack by a grouse hen in defense of her brood. Someone moving through the dense forest vegetation at that season is more likely to be concerned about fending off the swarms of mosquitos and deerflies, brushing against a hornets' nest,

overtaking a skunk, or stumbling over a branch or log hidden under the bracken ferns. Then, without warning, there is a sudden charge by an unseen animal making an assortment of hisses and squeals. First the flow of adrenaline prepares you to flee, if you can determine which direction is safe. But almost before you can react you realize that it is only a ruffed grouse hen, with her ruff erected and tail fanned to make her look as large as she can. As quickly as she charged, she retreats, giving a continuous sequence of calls to her chicks telling them to stay hidden.

This is an effective strategy, for during that momentary confusion of the hen's charge, the attention of the animal or person being charged is focused on her. In that moment, her brood scatters, crawling under leaves and branches, into ro-

By early July grouse chicks are shifting from a diet of animal matter to a menu of plant materials including strawberries and soft woodland sedges and grasses.

dent holes, or into bunches of grass over an area of several square yards. When the hen retreats, a potential predator is faced with the difficult task of finding even one of the hidden chicks.

Chick numbers diminish very rapidly through the early summer, and about 60 percent of the chicks hatched in early June have usually died by mid-August. Many of these losses are accidental. Chicks become separated from the hen and become chilled or drown by falling into water-filled holes. And many chicks fall prey to a large assortment of animals. Habitats that are good places for ruffed grouse to grow up in are also good places for many other animals, such as weasels, skunks, raccoons, and the occasional bobcat or fox passing through. Where people are living nearby, house cats and dogs running loose take their toll. Even red squirrels will not pass up an opportunity to eat a grouse chick if it finds one separated from the brood.

Broad-winged hawks and Cooper's or sharp-shinned hawks also find ruffed grouse brood habitat a fruitful place to hunt. These predators take an especially heavy toll when broods move across trails or into large openings to feed.

On the Cloquet study area, we have been unable to find any concrete evidence that cold, wet springs have a significant impact on brood survival and subsequent grouse numbers. Our evidence indicates that when grouse numbers are down in the fall, it is the result of events during the preceding winter -- or even a year earlier. This depression of numbers comes from a reduction in the reproductive potential of hens.

Some years, even when substantial numbers of chicks hatch, they have insufficient stamina to survive the first few days or weeks. Apparently there just was not enough of the essential nutrients in the egg to produce a strong, vigorous chick. Some of the most ideal spring seasons have been the years when early losses among broods were most severe. On the other hand, some other years having prolonged periods of cool, wet weather during May and June have proven to be among the most productive we've seen in northern Minnesota.

For example, there were 206 daylight hours of

*Brooding the anxious chicks becomes
increasingly difficult for the hen. Once on
the brood range, she apparently no longer
leads them, but tags along as lookout.*

low-temperature stress (below 60°F) during periods of prolonged wet weather in June 1967. For 36 hours, the temperature was below 45°F, yet this season was the turnaround year for the grouse population here, resulting in the upswing that led eventually to the 1971-72 high. The year that dampened that increase, though, was the following season, 1968, when there were 109 hours of low temperatures and wet conditions, and only two hours below 45°F. That winter was a hard one on ruffed grouse, with lower amounts of snowfall and a marked depression in aspen flower bud numbers. Although there seemed to be a good hatch of chicks that spring, and the weather in June was nearly ideal, the grouse population slumped.

Although the chicks may move a considerable distance from their nest site to a brood range, once they have reached their summer-long range, they spend the remainder of the summer foraging over an area of about 14 to 44 acres.

Available data suggests that broods tend to stay separated from one another, but that one or more broods may use different parts of the same brood range concurrently. There seems to be fairly continuous movement back and forth from one portion of a range to another [19].

Some interchange of chicks occurs when broods come into contact, or there may even be actual stealing or adoption of another hen's brood. At Cloquet, we have one definite record of a hen that either adopted or stole the brood of another hen. This banded hen had her nest destroyed by a predator, yet six weeks later she was seen about one-half mile from where her nest had been accompanying a brood of chicks about two-thirds grown. We have other instances of known intermingling of broods. These observations were based on birds marked individually with colored leg bands.

We know that broods can survive without the hen after they are eight-weeks old. A hen whose chicks hatched overnight on June 21-22, 1964, died on August 17, 1964, and at least two of her chicks survived to be shot by hunters during the 1964 fall hunting season.

By the time a grouse chick is 16 weeks-old, the young hens are as large or larger than their mothers, and range from 16.9 to 20.5 oz. in weight. The young males are nearly as large, or could even be larger, than their fathers and usually weigh about 18.3 to 22.6 oz. By this time, they look like adult grouse and one can be sure of their age only by examining the stage of molt on their wings, as described in the preceding chapter. At this age, they cannot be identified as being young by any other plumage characteristics or by their size.

In early fall, it is time for the grouse family to break up, with the young birds dispersing through the forest seeking a permanent place of their own. Once they've departed, the hen will return to the area where she spent the previous winter, probably not far from where she nested.

Chapter Seven

AUTUMN

F all on the North Shore of Lake Superior is the season when the brilliant colors of the forest and the clear blue of a clean sky are reflected in a multitude of ponds and lakes. The flame-colored leaves of the red maples and mountain ashes are emphasized by the golden masses of the aspens and birches. The cosmopolitan summer green truly goes out in a blaze of color. By mid-October, the leaves have fallen, the forest is in its winter condition, and the color contrasts are the rich greens of the cedars, firs, spruces, and pines and the graceful white-barked stems of the paper birches.

Here and there, clusters of bright red berries of the mountain ashes add bright splashes of color to the forest scene. This touch of color is temporary, however, as robins, grosbeaks, and waxwings compete vigorously for these succulent fruits. By the time the migrating songbirds have moved south, few berries remain on any berry-producing plant in northern Minnesota. But some years in the North Shore forests, there are so many mountain ash berries that the migratory fruit-eaters move south before all the berries are gone, so ruffed grouse have an opportunity to enjoy them into early winter. Occasionally they have to compete with black bears, for many of the bruin tribe like to feast on these fruits, too,

before going into winter hibernation.

For young grouse, the fall is a season of strife and searching for a secure home. For the adult males, the fall season is a prolonged period of strife. They must be continually vigilant, defending their activity centers from invasion by young males. Through drumming and other aggressive actions, they attempt to defend for themselves and a mate a covert that has sufficient resources to provide them with the necessities of life through the winter. Of course it is also a season when they should stay concealed from the many hunters looking for them. This includes both those carrying shotguns and the wild predators.

Young grouse search for a vacant covert where they can become established. Confrontation is frequent, especially for those young males moving through the better grouse coverts. There the most suitable activity centers are likely to be occupied by older drummers surviving from the previous season.

Although the established males drum irregularly during the fall, they may have to physically defend their territories against persistent young males from time to time. We don't often witness these confrontations between two males, or at least have the opportunity to see the outcome, but one October day I came upon two

During some autumns, moutain-ash berries are so numerous that even the migratory birds can't eat them all. Ruffed grouse can then enjoy the fruits into early winter.

males, both banded, in just such a situation. One was a 27-month old drummer, a surprising 1,640 feet from the primary log he had occupied for two years. The other bird was a young male, banded only 27 days earlier at a trap about 560 feet from where this dispute occurred. The young male was nearly 3.5 oz. lighter than the older male.

The two birds were standing almost breast to breast in the middle of a roadway, the old male facing away from his activity center. Neither bird had a spread tail or erected ruff, but both were standing as tall as they could stretch. There was no fighting or pecking, only maneuvering. The older male kept pressing forward, with each step his tail fanned slightly, and he forced the young male backwards. The older bird stepped forward first to one side of his adversary, then to the other, ever crowding the younger bird farther from the older bird's territory. After several minutes, the younger male turned and ran off into cover. The older male was evidently satisfied that he had prevailed and did not pursue.

Young males that have succeeded in finding a vacant activity center, or have occupied one they believe to be suitable, start expressing their dominance by mid-October. Some young male ruffed grouse are actively engaged in drumming activity by the time they are 18 to 20-weeks old.

Autumn is a season of strife for grouse as young males randomly disperse either into vacant activity centers . . .

. . . or into an area already dominated by an adult male with an aggressive determination to defend his territory against intruders.

This is also a period of heavy losses among young birds. Many of these dispersing birds move into places where the habitat is unsuitable for grouse. The inexperienced young birds become exceedingly vulnerable to predation. This season of random movement coincides with the period when a large number of young predators have been turned out on their own and are hungrily searching for anything they can catch. Many of these young predators are rather inept hunters, but by sheer numbers they take a heavy toll on the inexperienced young grouse.

Adult hens return from the ranges where they reared their broods to the area where they spent the previous winter, usually the general area where they nested several months earlier.

In the fall, food resources are normally quite abundant and present little problem. In most years, there is an abundance of fruits and berries available to grouse in most forest situations. The persistent fruits of low-growing bear-berries, bunchberry, and false lily-of-the-valley are particular favorites. The white fruits of the gray dogwood act like a magnet for ruffed grouse where it grows and attract the attention of both wild and human hunters as well. Where oaks grow, there are crops of acorns to be shared with squirrels and deer. By the way, often grouse benefit from deer feeding on the larger acorns, for they break them into smaller chunks that grouse can handle.

When rains are frequent and the forest is moist, there'll be many mushrooms, and ruffed grouse do like mushrooms, but they have to compete with red squirrels for these. Red squirrels collect mushrooms in the fall and place them in sunny sites where they will dry. Sometimes these rodents use ruffed grouse drumming logs for their "drying racks."

In the fall, as well as other seasons, grouse drumming logs are used by many animals besides the drummers. Not only do squirrels use them for drying mushrooms, but they commonly use them as the place to take pine cones apart, looking for seeds. Woodpeckers often work over drumming logs, looking for insects burrowing in the wood, and occasionally a log will be rolled over or torn apart by a bear seeking the large ants or termites that often live in logs. Quite frequently, the scattered feathers of a song-bird or fur of a squirrel, chipmunk, or snowshoe hare will show that a log has been used as a feeding perch by a raptor.

There are many evergreen, frost-resistant herbs available to ruffed grouse until snowfall. The leaves of clovers and strawberries are special favorites in the fall. I've also seen grouse crops filled with the yellowed, fallen leaves of aspen. Some grouse continue to feed on insects. So finding something to eat does not appear to be of much concern for ruffed grouse in the fall.

By early October, ruffed grouse are beginning

Autumn is also a period of heavy losses among young grouse, for dispersal coincides with a season-high presence of predators.

to sample, to varying degrees, some of the foods that will sustain them through the winter. Early in October, we'll find some grouse crops filled with aspen buds, hazel or birch catkins, and occasionally an alder catkin or two. These birds are beginning to feed on the foods that will be their almost exclusive diet once snow has buried the forest floor. Once winter snows begin to accumulate, the succulent greenery, and most of the fruits they used earlier, will not be available.

"EDGES" ARE DANGEROUS PLACES FOR GROUSE

Anyone who has been exposed to ideas concerning wildlife management, or tales of hunting, has surely heard about the "edge effect" and its importance to wildlife.

Aldo Leopold, the "Father of modern game management," was perhaps the first to dignify this concept by attaching some importance to it. In 1933, Leopold wrote [49]:

"Game is a phenomenon of edges. It occurs where the types of food and cover which it needs come together, i.e., where their edges meet...We do not understand the reason for all of these edge effects, but in those cases where we can guess the reason, it usually harks back either to the desirability of simultaneous access to more than one environmental type, or the greater richness of border vegetation, or both."

Since Leopold wrote this, edges have been the focus of much attention by wildlife managers. Considerable effort has gone into creating as much edge as possible for many wildlife species. Ruffed grouse have usually been included among the species for whom the development of a great deal of "edge" is supposedly beneficial.

However, when we take a closer look at what happens at the edges where ruffed grouse concentrate, and why the birds are there, the story takes a different slant. Actually, extensive use of forest edges by ruffed grouse provides the best indication of how unsatisfactory a forest habitat has become for these birds. When grouse must depend upon edges to find the resources they need,

Although autumn food resources are normally of great variety, by mid-October grouse are beginning to sample the basic foods that will sustain them through winter.

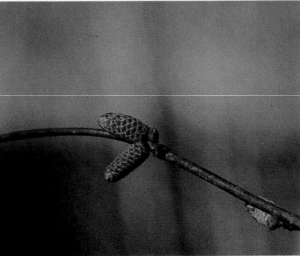

The white fruits of the gray dogwood act like a magnet for ruffed grouse in autumn. In turn, wild and human hunters are attracted to them as well.

Grouse must compete with red squirrels for delectable fall mushrooms which these rodents tend to collect and dry in sunny sites before eating.

it means that the rest of the forest is deficient in those resources, and the quality of the habitat has deteriorated to such a state that only a small portion remains acceptable.

This is a deadly situation for ruffed grouse. When they are forced to concentrate in a narrow corridor along the edge of a forest, the stage is set for excessive losses to predation or sport hunting. Predators and hunters know precisely where the grouse are going to be, and can work those narrow corridors repeatedly until the population is nearly, if not completely, decimated.

On the other hand, if good-quality cover is uniformly spread over several acres, the grouse become widely dispersed throughout the cover, and predators, as well as hunters, soon become discouraged trying to find the grouse. This is especially so in the most secure habitats where there are usually only two or three grouse scattered in an area of eight to 10 acres. In this situation, for every square foot a grouse may occupy, there are about 145,000 square feet with *no* grouse. The chances of finding a grouse under these conditions are pretty slim.

This somewhat unconventional outlook is a result of watching ruffed grouse abandon the edges they traditionally used in response to the development of blocks of better cover following commercial logging or clear-cutting designed to improve grouse habitat.

In the early days of the Cloquet study, ruffed grouse occurred most often on edges [15], right where most published studies of ruffed grouse

habitat use said they should be. That relationship with edges, which also was associated with relatively sparse grouse numbers, did not change much until 1970. In the meantime, sapling aspen stands developed on several parts of the Cloquet Forest following clear-cutting of mixed pine-aspen forests from 1958 to 1963. In 1970 and later, ruffed grouse ceased to use the edges they had used for so long, and we started finding them in unexpected densities in the aspen saplings. In 1970, for example, 49 percent of the breeding grouse were concentrated on 14 percent of the forest, on 450 acres of seven to 25 year-old aspen, at densities of 10 breeding males per 100 acres.

In 1972, with more breeding grouse on this area than had been recorded here since Ralph King worked here in the early 1930's, many of the coverts used during the preceding decade were vacant. But drumming males were crowded into the young aspen coverts at densities of 22 birds per 100 acres. In addition, for every 2.3 males we knew was using a drumming log, there was another male quietly biding his time, waiting for a vacancy to occur [27]. But these non-drumming males waited for vacancies in the new aspen coverts rather than using the vacant, little-changed coverts that had been quite acceptable to grouse a few years earlier.

Attempting to evaluate ruffed grouse habitat preferences or needs in forests that have not undergone significant disturbance within the last 20 years is liable to lead to erroneous conclusions concerning their basic cover needs.

Classic forest edges can actually become death traps to grouse when the birds must concentrate along a narrow corridor. Grouse cover needs are best suited when blocks of quality habitat are uniformly spread throughout an area.

Chapter Eight

DISPERSAL

As in human families, when young ruffed grouse are fully grown, most of them leave the home they've known to seek a place of their own to spend the rest of their lives. This usually happens when they are about 15 or 16-weeks old. On the North Shore this begins about the middle of September.

The dispersal of young ruffed grouse from their summer brood ranges occurs as two distinct events [20]. First comes the breakup of the family, when the young grouse moves some distance away from the cover where it spent the summer with its mother and siblings. Then a few days later, dispersal begins in earnest when the young grouse move toward an unknown destination.

Generally, the young males are the first to disperse. In northern Minnesota, their most extensive movement occurs during the last two weeks of September, although they are still moving around quite a lot in early October. The young females begin their major journey about the first of October and have generally reached their destination 15 to 20 days later.

In southern Indiana, where ruffed grouse clutches hatch a week or two earlier than in northern Minnesota, the timing of the brood breakup and fall dispersal coincides with these events farther north [3].

Most of the young males become established on drumming logs within a mile of their brood range, with a few moving as far as three miles. Most young hens move from three or four times farther than the young males before they settle into the covert that will be their winter home; some young hens in northern Minnesota have moved as far as 8.6 to 10.4 miles.

Although young females tend to end their fall dispersal farther from brood ranges than the males, both sexes appear to be equally mobile. The difference between the apparent greater mobility of young females compared to young males reflects the tendency for the hens to move in the same general direction that they were headed when dispersal began. Young cocks, on the other hand, may move out then return to the vicinity of their brood range. This pattern of tentative movement away from the brood range and return may occur two or three times, until the young male eventually finds his drumming log. A young cock appears to be more reluctant to leave home and evidently prefers to occupy an activity center near his juvenile home range if he can find a satisfactory vacant site.

But even all the young females don't move too far. We have records of hens rearing their broods in the same alder lowlands where they grew up a

Most dispersal movement is done by daylight walking. A young grouse may quickly but cautiously move a few thousand feet, linger for several days, then move on.

Foliage is still dense enough for suitable concealment when dispersal begins, but autumn is brief on the North Shore and frosts soon deny ruffed grouse of that security.

A young grouse occupying marginal habitat has slim prospects of survival. As much as one percent of the population perishes daily during dispersal.

year or two earlier.

Nor is early fall brood breakup inevitable. There are records of broods of banded ruffed grouse remaining together into mid-October, and one brood was still intact in mid-January before dispersing to the widely-scattered sites where they were found three months later.

Most of the dispersal movement is done in spurts by grouse walking during daylight. A dispersing young grouse will quickly move a few thousand feet, remain in a small area for a few days, then move on quickly to another area. This pattern may be repeated three or four times before they reach their eventual destination [20]. Most frequently, the period of movement coincides with the passage of a cold weather frontal system and a spell of stormy weather.

A dispersing ruffed grouse can cover a considerable amount of ground in a short period of time. In 1964, one radio-tagged young male at Cloquet walked about three miles in three days, making only two short flights [20].

When ruffed grouse are walking through the forest, they remain ever alert to possible danger. When passing stumps, large trees, or objects that might conceal a crouching predator, they allow enough space to give them the opportunity to escape. When they have to pass by piles of branches on the ground, they'll often go over the pile, rather than around or through it. Brush piles are not good cover for ruffed grouse, but they do provide great cover for animals that eat grouse. When a ruffed grouse approaches a log or pile of logs, it usually hops up on the log and walks along the top a bit before dropping off the other side.

Fall dispersal is a dangerous period for ruffed grouse. These inexperienced young birds are abandoning the guidance of their mother and the comfortable security of a familiar brood range to strike out through unfamiliar country seeking a covert that will provide them with their lifelong needs. When they begin their dispersal, the foliage is still dense and concealment is good. But environmental conditions change quickly during this period. Fall frosts crumple the vegetation, and when the leaves fall, these young birds suddenly lose much of the security they have enjoyed until now.

Also, this is the season when thousands of hawks and owls that nested farther north are moving south enroute to their wintering grounds. The season's young bobcat kittens, fox pups, young skunks, and other predators are also dispersing. This means that while inexperienced young grouse are moving through unfamiliar habitats, there is a major movement of hungry predators looking for any animal that happens to be in the wrong place at the right time. The level of predation is very high in the fall. This is the season when many ruffed grouse die.

Studies elsewhere indicate that young ruffed grouse die at a rate of about one percent of the population each day during the period of fall dispersal [16,55,64].

This is also the season for the annual hunt of grouse in Minnesota, but in the wilderness of the North Shore forests, predation by humans is probably relatively unimportant as a factor affecting grouse numbers.

Fall dispersal is an important part of the ruffed grouse's biological processes, and serves two very important functions. First, it is the mechanism by which members of a family become widely scattered. Since young hens generally settle into home ranges quite remote from their male broodmates, a mixing of the gene pool is assured with little likelihood of sisters mating with brothers.

Secondly, fall dispersal is the mechanism that assures that when new habitats are created, by whatever means, they will be promptly occupied when they develop into coverts suitable for ruffed grouse. These new coverts may have resulted from a fire, windstorm, flood, landslide, or logging activity.

When an opening has been created by a fire, windstorm or logging, it takes about eight to 10 years until a clear-cut aspen stand develops into satisfactory ruffed grouse cover. We often find that dispersing young ruffed grouse begin "testing" the quality of developing areas several

DISPERSAL AND DEPLETED COVERTS

Although the randomness of fall dispersal by young grouse is advantageous for the species, it oftentimes works to the disadvantage of grouse hunters. This is particularly true in regions where access is limited to the proximity of roads and trails, leaving large tracts of wild country seldom penetrated by grouse hunters. In these situations, dispersal, is as likely to take young grouse deeper into "refuges of inaccessibility" as towards the places where they are accessible. If hunting depletes the grouse population in accessible areas, the random nature of fall dispersal means that depleted coverts may not be restocked by young grouse. This is particularly true where hunting continues long after dispersal has ceased in late October or early November.

years before the coverts have developed sufficiently to provide them with winter-long protection. It is not unusual to find drumming logs being selected by pioneering young males three or four years after clear-cutting, with the birds using these sites in the fall and then either being killed or moving to more secure sites before the next spring.

This scenario may be repeated several times over a period of years as the cover develops until it finally becomes adequate. Then a fall occupant finally survives the winter and becomes a part of the next spring's breeding population. From then on, for the next 10 to 15 years, fall occupation and overwinter survival on the site is the rule.

Dispersing young males have to contend with surviving older males occupying the best drumming logs in the better-quality habitats. A major reason for fall drumming by the old males is to express their dominance and to discourage the

The classic term, "crazy-flight," wive's-tales notwithstanding,
appears to be strictly a matter of frightened young grouse
escaping a danger from behind without regard for
the trees, buildings, and other obstacles ahead.

intrusion by young males looking for a vacant drumming log. Since fall drumming serves to disperse young grouse and reduces the likelihood of numbers exceeding local food and cover resources, this serves another very important biological function -- it assures that grouse in good coverts will have a maximum likelihood of surviving until next spring.

During fall dispersal, the most numerous grouse may not be found in the best grouse coverts. As noted earlier, territorial males surviving from spring are defending many of the best coverts in fall against the intrusion of other grouse. This means that the more gregarious, non-territorial, young grouse are likely to be found in poorer habitats. But if the habitat is so poor that prior occupants haven't survived to defend it against intrusion by young birds, the newcomers will also be short-lived.

On the other hand, these less-secure habitats may be the best place for sportsmen to hunt. Ruffed grouse in these coverts are mostly young birds, still sociable enough to occur in groups, but still not experienced enough to run or fly while approaching danger is still a safe distance away. And as we said earlier, each of these young grouse likes to decide for itself whether or not to flush, providing a hunter with several opportunities for a shot as several birds get up as singles.

In the fall, grouse habitat should not be judged on the basis of bird abundance. The coverts where grouse are most abundant in the fall are often rather unsatisfactory places for winter survival.

Anyone that is familiar with the classic grouse literature has certainly encountered the term "crazy-flight." In fact, they may even have read some fairly-lengthy articles attempting to explain this curious behavior.

"Crazy-flight" is not difficult to understand or explain. It probably seldom has anything to do with intoxicated grouse, worms, or any other abnormal conditions. It seems to be strictly a matter of frightened young grouse, startled by something, being more concerned by what is behind than what is ahead. As a result, in its panic, it flies into trees, buildings, or whatever else may happen to be in the way.

The grouse mentioned earlier that hit a tree so hard on the Cloquet Forest was flushed from a lawn moments before. And in Michigan a number of years ago, Tom Prawdzik saw a grouse pursued by a Cooper's hawk plunge into the snow and bury itself only eight feet from where Tom stood [58].

Nor is it surprising that grouse fly into glass windows. Certainly a wild, young grouse has never had an experience with something it could see through but couldn't fly through. This must be particularly confusing when there are two windows on opposite sides of a room, giving the appearance of a way through a building.

Working with trapped ruffed grouse, we have had instances when released birds have flown into the first tree they encountered. Sometimes they collided with trees as far as 100 feet from the release site. This has occurred frequently enough that we no longer release grouse into full flight; we always place them in heavy cover of some sort so they have to either walk away, or at least settle down and become better oriented before they fly. This practice has eliminated handling losses from that cause.

Chapter Nine

WINTER

Winter here is a quiet season. Most of the songbirds have flown to warmer regions, though for some, this *is* a warmer region. Flocks of redpolls swarm and chatter among the birches and alders, feeding on seeds still held in the catkins. Crossbills use their uniquely-shaped bills to pry open the cones of the pines and other evergreens and use a rasp-surfaced tongue to extract the seeds. The vari-colored pine grosbeaks give a clear, almost bell-like call from the tops of trees while they move through the forest seeking fruits and buds. Brilliantly colored high-bush cranberries are particularly attractive to them and are usually plentiful because few other animals relish the tart taste of these bright red berries.

Even the tumbling waterfalls are stilled in the dead of winter. The big lake remains restless, piling ice upon shoreline rocks, but seldom becoming totally stilled by a solid cover of ice.

When environmental conditions are favorable, winter is the best season of the year for ruffed grouse. But to be favorable means having a winter-long abundance of deep, soft snow and sufficient high-quality food resources nearby. Ruffed grouse can properly be called "chionophiles," [17] or "snow-lovers," for winter can be the one season when they are able to relax and have a comparatively serene life.

Ruffed grouse move about more in winter than at other seasons, but for the most part remain within a fairly confined area. Males generally remain within a 530-yard radius of their drumming logs. Earlier we noted that they return to their drumming logs from time to time during the winter. This is especially true in those winters when there is not much snow and the forms of logs remain distinct in the shallow snow. As long as the bird can find a site that gives him a superior position in relation to his surroundings, he will continue to use his log. Drumming is infrequent in winter, but does occur on an occasional warmer day.

Even though there may be little drumming activity, defense of the territory continues unabated. Males protecting their activity centers continue to display against unwelcome intruders. Occasionally, they may be seen in full display on the snow, but more often their tracks are seen where they have strutted along a territorial boundary, leaving conspicuous drag marks from their rigidly-extended wings. Usually, the tracks of the grouse against whom the display was mounted parallel the drag marks of the defending bird.

The females are somewhat more mobile at this

During winters of heavy snow and abundant food resources, grouse can relax and lead a relatively serene life.

Males continue to defend their territories throughout winter. Occasionally one is seen in full display . . .

. . . but more often only the tracks are left, indicating where a bird strutted along his territorial boundary leaving conspicuous marks from his rigid, extended wings.

season, ranging over the territories of at least a couple of males. The winter home ranges of hens cover about 20 to 30 acres. They move back and forth from one part to another, depending upon their need for the resources that the different parts of their winter range may provide [8].

Winter is the season when flight is a critical part of a grouse's activity. When more than three or four inches of soft snow lies on the ground, ruffed grouse must fly to get around, unless the snow has a hard crust. Then they have other problems.

In the fall, horny growths develop on the feet of ruffed grouse. These have often been called "snow-shoes," but this is as much a misnomer as the name "partridge" for these birds. When the snow is soft, these growths, or "pectin," do not provide much support, and the birds still sink deeply when trying to walk through it. But these growths are probably very important to the feeding grouse climbing around on the ice or snow-covered branches of an aspen searching for flower buds or fruit, providing additional grip, like tire chains on slippery surfaces.

Although winter can be a season for relaxation when conditions are good, it is still a season when survival is uppermost among ruffed grouse concerns. Survival means living in a habitat where the birds have an adequate food resource, protection from heat loss to the environment, and protection from predation.

Thermal protection can be of two kinds. The most satisfactory thermal protection available to North Shore ruffs in winter is an accumulation of deep, powdery snow. The snow must be about 10-inches deep to provide a satisfactory burrow-roost. There should be at least three or four inches of snow over the bird, and the snow must be of such a character that it does not collapse behind a burrowing bird -- a collapsed snow-burrow pinpoints the location of a roosting grouse.

A ruffed grouse snow-burrow may be no more than a yard long, marking the path where the bird dived into the snow, roosted, and then burst out the next day. On other occasions, the bird may burrow through the snow for 15 to 20 feet,

The flanges developing on the feet of grouse have been called "snow-shoes." These growths provide additional grip for birds climbing on icy branches in search of food.

When walking, ruffed grouse still sink deeply
into soft snow despite those "snow-shoe"
flanges on their feet.

zig-zagging back and forth.

Snow-burrow roosting is by no means unique to ruffed grouse. The closely related ptarmigans living in the Arctic and high Western mountains roost in snow-burrows whenever possible. Even the large Eurasian capercaillie depends upon snow-burrows for winter roosting across the northern part of its range. It takes three feet of soft snow to provide secure burrows for "capers," the largest of the grouse.

Since grouse usually plunge headlong into a snow-burrow from full flight, a grouse is least likely to be injured if it can dive into the snow in sites where there are no fallen branches or logs on the ground. This is why snow-burrows are often seen in trails and roadways and around the edges of open, grassy fields. A recently-burned forest, where all the downed branches and other woody material has been removed, provides a safer place for burrow-roosting than a forest where many downed limbs and branches may lie concealed under the snow.

A grouse in a snow-burrow has two definite advantages over a grouse roosting anywhere else in the winter. One obvious advantage is concealment from predators, particularly the raptors searching for a brown body against white snow. A grouse that has entered the snow, making a hole that is no more than four or five inches in diameter and then burrowed for some distance, is well concealed from most searching predators.

Snow depth must be about 10 inches to provide a satisfactory burrow-roost. A collapsed burrow pinpoints the location of a roosting grouse to predators.

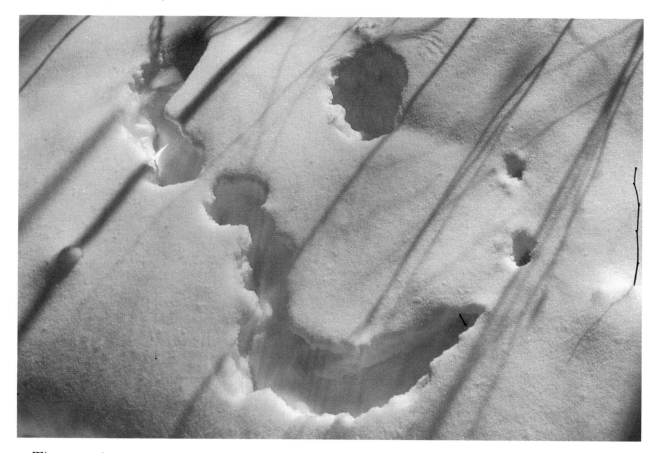

The second benefit for the bird in the snow is the relative warmth it enjoys there. Temperatures in the snow in hardwood forests in northern Minnesota seldom drop below about 20°F, which is no colder than many nights here in early spring. A ruffed grouse in a snow-burrow is essentially spending its winter nights in a spring-like environment.

This 20°F-temperature figure is particularly important to ruffed grouse. This temperature appears to be the lower critical temperature for these birds during the winter [60]. The insulation provided by their feathers becomes insufficient to keep a resting ruffed grouse warm when temperatures drop below 20°F. At lower temperatures, the bird must speed up its body metabolism to keep warm. Ruffed grouse do not have the compact, dense plumage that characterizes some other members of their family, and therefore they are less well-adapted for exposure to cold weather. Using snow-burrows is their best means of coping with this deficiency. The white-tailed ptarmigan,

on the other hand, has much more dense plumage than ruffed grouse, and their lower critical temperature is about -29° F in winter [74]. But they, too, use snow-burrows as often as they can.

When they cannot use a snow-burrow, ruffed grouse will roost in a "snow-bowl" or in a conifer. The snow-bowl is where the bird makes a deep, nest-like depression in the surface of the snow so that only the upper surface of its body is exposed. The conifer may be a balsam fir, pine, spruce, or cedar. While ambient air temperatures in conifer tree-roosts are colder than in a snow-burrow, or even a snow-bowl roost, the overhead cover still reduces radiant heat loss to the night sky, so coniferous cover provides a grouse with some protection from heat loss during periods of winter cold.

Robert Brander at Cloquet studied the radiant heat loss ruffed grouse had to cope with during a cold December night [8]. This is an expression of the rate of heat loss to the night sky from a warm body. He found that the radiant temperature in

The grouse most likely to survive winter are those that can consistently burst from adequate snow-burrows to a nearby food source, minimizing exposure to predation.

an open site was about 54°F colder than the ambient -- prevailing -- air temperature. At this same time, the radiant temperature under a coniferous canopy was nearly the same as the ambient air temperature. When a cloud cover moved in, the radiant temperature in the open site rose to approximately that of the ambient air.

In spite of the frequent use of pines, firs, cedars, or spruce by these birds for roosting, coniferous cover is not a good substitute for snow-burrows. The years when ruffed grouse in northern Minnesota have had to make heavy use of needle-leaved cover for roosting have been years when the grouse population suffered marked declines. One problem with evergreen cover is that it provides excellent concealment for the raptors that are most successful in preying on ruf-

fed grouse. Grouse that make consistent use of this type of protection have much less likelihood of surviving.

In questioning the value of conifers as grouse cover, I should stress that it is not a black and white case. The structure of the spruces, firs, cedars, and probably hemlock is such that these species provide poorer cover for raptors than the "high-tree" pines, with their lower branches shed. Young pines also provide secure ruffed grouse cover for perhaps 15 to 20 years. The problem is, though, that the pine stand is not likely to be cut and replanted when it is only 20 years old. More likely, it will dominate the site for 60 to 80 years, making the site untenable for grouse for more than a half century.

Even the spruce-fir cover decreases in value as

When unable to use snow-burrows, ruffed grouse may roost in a conifer. Such cover provides only minimum protection against radiant heat loss and avian predators.

Evergreen cover also conceals the same predators from which the grouse attempt to hide. Birds frequently using this type of protection are likely to perish before spring.

it becomes older. One 154-acre parcel on the Cloquet Forest has a textbook interspersion of spruce and fir conifer cover, with mature aspen amply distributed over the area. In 1961, this area supported 11 males, a density of 7.1 per 100 acres. But as the conifers have grown older, grouse numbers have steadily declined until in 1983 there were only six birds on the area, 3.9 per 100 acres. So far, I have not seen a situation where the overall density, or survival, of ruffed grouse living in association with coniferous cover has equalled the density and survival of these grouse in young aspen away from conifers.

The ideal winter for ruffed grouse is the one we consider a "tough one." That is, the winter when there are 10 inches or more of soft, powdery snow on the ground by Thanksgiving, and no rain or

At Cloquet a stable, high grouse population
was at least partly the result of birds living
among moderately dense aspen saplings
offering little access to raptors.

CLIMATIC FACTORS INFLUENCING WINTER GROUSE SURVIVAL

Having made several comments about wintering conditions for ruffed grouse in this region, I will describe the characteristics of favorable and unfavorable seasons, and show how one contrasts with the other. Our definition of winter is from the time snow cover becomes persistent in the fall until it has melted in the spring. For examples, I'll compare the favorable winter of 1969-70 to 1972-73 when grouse numbers plummeted. From 1969 to 1970, adult male survival was 61 percent, and the breeding male population on the Cloquet Forest increased from 71 to 106 birds. Conversely, from 1972 to 1973, adult male survival was only 31 percent and the population declined from 187 to 101 breeding males.

If we consider mean temperatures, there was not much difference between the 13.6°F winter-long mean for 1969-70 and the 18.9°F for 1972-73. If anything, from the standpoint of winter-long mean temperatures, the year when the population declined seemed the more favorable. The mean minimum for the year of rising grouse numbers was 2.7°F, and during the declining year 10.9°F. The difference between the years becomes evident when snow conditions are considered.

In 1969-70, snow cover lasted 149 days, from November 11 to April 10, while in 1972-73 snow covered the ground for 130 days, from November 14 to March 27. In the good year, there were 66 days of satisfactory conditions for snow-burrow roosting, and only eight days in 1972-73.

In terms of temperature stress, in 1969-70 ruffed grouse had to endure 668 hours of temperatures below 20°F, and 135 hours of temperatures below zero when they could not burrow-roost. In 1972-73, they had to cope with 1,114 hours below 20°F, and 273 hours below zero when they could not burrow-roost. Finally, during the favorable year, aspen flower buds were readily available and heavily used. In 1972-73, aspen buds were still fairly abundant, but ruffed grouse made little use of the buds this season.

above-freezing temperatures until well into March. Daytime temperatures should remain in the 20's, dropping to the zero or subzero range overnight to maintain light, powdery snow.

All snow on the North Shore is not equally acceptable as cover for ruffed grouse. One common misconception is that ruffed grouse burrow into snow drifts. But, in truth, snow that has formed drifts tends to be too firmly-packed for ruffed grouse to use. They prefer it lying undisturbed where it has fallen.

The best site is on a level or south-facing exposure in a hardwood forest where the snow is fully exposed to the sun all day. In these sites, the heat from the sun slowly penetrates the snow so that the maximum daily temperature is attained in a snow-burrow six inches under the surface about 1 a.m. at night. Then, as the snow loses heat to the environment, the temperature begins to drop, reaching its lowest point 12 hours later, shortly after noon. Since this fluctuation amounts to only two or three degrees, this daily change is of little importance to the roosting grouse, especially when compared to what is happening at the surface of the snow or in the trees overhead.

In well-protected tree roosts in dense balsam fir, the daily temperature range may be as much as 36° with mid-winter temperatures varying from 2°F at midday to as cold as -26°F by sunrise the next morning. Often there are 30 to 40 degrees difference between the temperature a grouse is en-

Grouse populations can be hard-hit during winters of moderate snow cover with intermittent rains or above freezing temperatures.

joying in a snug snow-burrow and the temperature at the surface of the snow. If that bird were roosting in a fir or spruce tree, it would be as much as 10 degrees colder than at the surface of the snow during the coldest days of winter.

Ruffed grouse have another advantage on the North Shore and across some of their Canadian range that they don't have farther south. This country, with short summers and cold water, has an extensive network of bogs. Many of these consist of layers of the partially-decayed remains of trees, sedges, and other vegetation floating on water. This mat may be several feet thick and feel quite solid to walk on. Often these floating mats are covered with forests of black spruce, white cedar, and tamarack. But there may be many feet of water between the underside of the mat and the soil at the bottom of these extinct lakes. Occasionally, you'll find a situation on a bog where waves can be made in the water under the mat by jumping up and down, and you can watch the trees sway back and forth as the waves move outward from under the mat.

This mass of water is a great heat reservoir. Snow lying on these bogs, especially on open bogs or muskeg, does not get as cold as it does on upland sites. The temperature at the surface of a bog under two or three feet of snow may remain within three or four degrees below freezing, when it may be as low as -30 to -40°F at the upper surface of the snow. Heat from the bog radiates up through the snow, so grouse roosting deep over muskeg are enjoying even warmer nighttime temperatures than those using upland sites nearby.

When a period of warm weather occurs and the snow becomes crusted, the best thing for grouse is another snowstorm depositing at least another eight inches of snow on top of the crust. Probably the worst thing that can happen to these birds in mid-winter is to have a fall of five or six inches of fine snow on a hard crust. This is just enough to allow a bird to dive into the snow and even burrow through it for some distance, but not enough to maintain a covering over the bird. The grouse ends up spending its time like the legendary ostrich with its head in the sand. While the head and foreparts of the bird are

covered, its rump and tail remain exposed, conspicuous targets for predators.

When there are only three or four inches of fresh snow covering a crust, it is not uncommon to see where a grouse attempted to dive into a burrow, skidded along the surface for several feet, stood up and shook itself, and then walked away to roost elsewhere.

In late winter, when the warmer sun begins changing the physical structure of the snow from densely-packed, fine snow-crystals of winter to the coarser, springtime ice crystals, ruffed grouse sometimes dig themselves into burrows. They cannot penetrate this coarser snow by diving into it as they do earlier in the winter, but can scratch their way through the coarse surface crystals and then make a satisfactory burrow once under the surface crust.

The least desirable conditions for grouse in terms of weather are the winters of sustained bitter cold with little or no snow cover. These conditions place ruffed grouse in double jeopardy. The bitter cold and lack of burrowing snow exposes the birds to a continuous drain of their physiological resources. They must maintain a high level of metabolic activity to maintain body heat, which means burning their body's energy reserves at an accelerated pace.

To maintain this pace, they must process an increased volume of food which means spending more time feeding. Since most winter-time feeding means exposure to chilling breezes and increased risk of predation, the hazard is multiplied. Also, insufficient snow cover means the resting grouse are without the security afforded by a blanket of snow. Although they may make extensive use of coniferous cover under these conditions, this does not really offset the lack of good burrowing snow.

Equally bad are the winters of moderately heavy snow cover and intermittent periods of rainy weather or temperatures above freezing. These conditions keep a crust on the snow that grouse are unable to penetrate. Although we see and hear comments about ruffed grouse being trapped under a crust or being killed by diving

A ruffed grouse usually plunges from full flight into a snow-burrow to spend the winter night in a warm environment. In the morning it bursts into the air with rapid wingstrokes.

into crusted snow, this seems to be uncommon. In all the years of research at Cloquet, we have yet to see where this has occurred.

One of the most severe tests of this element occurred at Cloquet from March 2-4, 1966. On the 3rd, nearly six inches of snow fell during a storm coming from the northeast off Lake Superior. After dark, when grouse should have gone to roost in burrows in this deep, fresh snow, the wind shifted to the southeast. The precipitation turned to freezing rain, and nearly a half-inch of blue ice covered the fresh snow. Still later that night, the wind switched to the northwest as a deep, low-pressure center passed over the Head-of-the-Lakes, and another four inches of fine, dry snow blown by a bitter wind blasting out of Canada covered the ice layer.

It was several weeks after that storm before we saw a grouse, and initially it appeared that the population had been decimated. But by early April, grouse were again being seen as frequently as before the storm, and eventually the winter of 1966 proved to be the turn-around season for that cyclic low. The grouse population began its upswing in 1966 to the highest level seen here since

the early 1950's.

In spite of the seemingly fatal combination of ideal burrowing snow early in the evening, later covered by an ice layer so hard that it required a hard blow with a shovel to break through it, we were unable to find any evidence of grouse mortality. In fact, to the contrary, overwinter survival among banded, adult male ruffed grouse was better than usual. Sixty percent of the banded drummers survived from 1965 to 1966 in contrast to survival of only 33 to 45 percent during the preceding three winters.

When the snowmobile craze hit, we often heard people expressing concern about grouse being run over and killed while in their burrows. We know of occasional cases when this did happen.

As the snow was melting in the spring of 1974, a member of the "drumming log" crew at Cloquet found two dead grouse close together along a woods road heavily used by snowmobiles. Both birds had crops full of aspen flower buds and little food material in their digestive tracts. This indicated that they had finished their evening meal and plunged into the snow only a short time

before being run over and killed.

But this incident can not be projected to make a case for indicting the snowmobile as a hazard to the grouse population. These birds were wintering in a forest stand where the odds were against their surviving. It was a 50-year old northern hardwood forest with many scattered pines and balsam fir. Even though ample food was available to grouse, the cover was more in favor of grouse predators. In the spring, there were seldom more than four breeding grouse in that 88-acre forest tract, proof of the inadequacy of the site.

However, grouse living in low-quality coverts do show a tendency to burrow-roost in trails and woods roads where they are more likely to be run over. This danger only exists early in the season, for once the trail has been used by a snowmobile, the snow would be too compacted for grouse to use it unless a substantial amount of new snow falls.

Again, quality of cover is important. In truly good ruffed grouse cover, the stems of trees and brush are too close together to permit the passage of a snowmobile. Even cross-country skiers have difficulty penetrating this cover, and someone on snowshoes has to be pretty agile to move through good habitat.

The matter of food resources will be discussed in the next chapter. The availability of food and cover are interacting facets of the grouse story, and the most successful birds are the ones that are able to fly directly from an adequate food resource to an adequate cover resource with a minimal of exposure to predation.

Chapter Ten

GROUSE FOODS & FEEDING

Ol' Ruff is an herbivore, and a browsing herbivore at that, right along with deer and moose. For most of their lives, the diet of ruffed grouse consists of the leaves and buds of plants. Like bears, they tend to be quite opportunistic in their feeding and will consume fruits, berries, and nuts, and, occasionally even snakes, salamanders, and frogs. But a meat diet is fairly uncommon. Mushrooms are fairly important in their diet in the fall.

Although ruffed grouse have a muscular stomach or gizzard similar to that of chickens, pheasants, and quail, seeds are not as important to them. It appears that most seeds that ruffed grouse ingest pass through their digestive system unaltered. In the fall, we commonly find the soft seeds of plants such as roses, mountain ash, sarsaparilla, false lily-of-the-valley, bunchberry, and the harder seeds of the dogwoods, thornapple, and cherries in the droppings beside drumming logs; these seeds are remarkably intact and are readily identifiable. In early summer, we have found the seeds of mountain ash germinating in piles of grouse droppings beside drumming logs, and this may account for the clumps of these shrubs. Ruffed grouse must play an important role in distributing the seeds of plants whose seeds would be too heavy to become widely distributed on their own.

Ruffed grouse are fairly catholic in their choice of foods during the summer and fall. Many fleshy-leafed or fruit-bearing plants are used at this season. In fact, a food-habits study of ruffed grouse during the summer, or the fall hunting season, is more likely to be useful as an inventory of fleshy-leafed and fruit-producing plants in a region than an indication of the foods that are important to ruffed grouse.

In regions where continuous winter snow cover is part of the winter ecology for grouse, these birds become very limited in their choice of food. It was long believed that since ruffed grouse feed on the buds and twigs of trees and shrubs, a shortage of adequate food through the winter would be unlikely. But this observation is not factual. In northern Minnesota, for a period of five to six months, they became almost exclusively florivorous, -- "flower-eaters" -- feeding almost exclusively upon the flower buds of a few forest trees and shrubs. The most important of these foods resources across the primary range of ruffed grouse are the flower buds of the male aspens or "popple." Dr. Frederick Greeley in New England called them "Popple Partridges"[22].

The male, or "staminate," flower buds of the aspens are almost the size of a kernel of corn.

Ruffed grouse ingest seeds, but their digestive system passes them essentially unaltered to the forest floor to germinate.

In early summer, we have found the seeds of mountain-ash germinating in piles of grouse droppings.

Ruffed grouse must play an important role in distributing the seeds too heavy to scatter widely on their own.

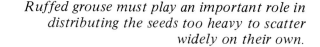

These buds develop in the leaf axils of new growth in late June and July and are available to grouse in the upper branches of the aspen all winter. The male aspen flower bud is relatively rich in nutrients such as protein, fats, and minerals. This, together with the bud's ready accessibility on rigid stems, makes it a most important food resource.

It should be pointed out that the aspens are particularly valuable as wildlife habitat due to some unusual traits. First, they most often grow as clones, with interconnecting root systems that may cover several acres. Secondly, aspens are either male or female, and all the trees in a clone are of the same sex.

In contrast to the size of the male bud, the female flower bud is a small, inconspicuous, nutrient-poor bud, seldom used by ruffed grouse. However, the green, beaded, seed-producing catkins, that develop about the same time as the leaves, are taken by the grouse for the short time they are available [73].

The idea that aspen is especially important to ruffed grouse is not new or limited to Minnesota. People interested in ruffed grouse identified aspen buds as being a particularly important food for ruffed grouse at least a half-century ago, although they failed to recognize that the male flower bud is most often used. Leon Kelso found aspen buds especially important to New York ruffed grouse in 1935 [42], and Charles Brown in Maine listed aspen as the most important winter food for ruffed grouse there in 1946 [10].

Summarizing a long-term study of ruffed grouse in New York, Dr. Gardiner Bump said:
"The large buds, long catkins, and tough leaves set on the stout twigs of the aspens (Populus) are particular favorites even when other food is abundant." [12]

A 1952 Wisconsin study found aspen buds to be particularly important to ruffed grouse and were used out of proportion to their availability in the forest [68]. A later Pennsylvania study also showed that aspen buds were consumed out of proportion to their availability [4]. This study was the first to call attention to the close correspondence between the distribution of aspen and ruffed grouse in North America. But it is interesting to note that a map in the classic 1947 report upon the New York grouse study shows the highest densities of ruffed grouse concentrated in that part of North America where aspen is most prevalent in the forest [12].

Aspen flower buds were found to be important to ruffed grouse in central Alberta, Canada, [14] and aspen catkins were being heavily used by ruffed grouse in southeastern Ohio in the

A "popple partridge" living up to its nickname.

mid-1970's [67]. A study of grouse feeding in the Wasatch Mountains in Utah showed aspen buds to be important, but it failed to distinguish the type of buds being eaten [57]. The male flower buds of another poplar, the black cottonwood, is an especially important food resource for ruffed grouse in western Washington [9].

In the early 1970's, Richard Huempfner made an especially detailed study of ruffed grouse use of aspen on the Cedar Creek Natural History Area north of Minneapolis, expanding on the work done at Cloquet in the 1960's [37].

The characteristics of aspen identified by Dr. Bump make this tree especially important to ruffed grouse. The twigs producing flower buds are stout enough to allow grouse to move around on them and feed with a minimum of wing motion and the accompanying loss of body heat and energy. There are normally five to eight male flower buds on a twig, permitting a grouse to feed rapidly and efficiently -- we have observed grouse taking more than 47 bites a minute. At this rate, it takes only 15 to 20 minutes for feeding grouse to fill their crops with about three ounces of flower buds, the usual evening meal. The quantity of this one meal for a ruffed grouse is equivalent to a 150-pound person eating 27 pounds of food at one sitting.

Throughout the winter, ruffed grouse normally feed twice a day, once about sunrise and again in the evening. If it is bitterly cold, they may forego the morning meal and remain in a snow-burrow until late in the afternoon, but the evening meal is always taken. During periods of extreme cold, ruffed grouse may be feeding in mid-afternoon, but usually not until sunset. Often the birds will begin gathering in the aspens a little while before sunset and either rest or perhaps engage in some chasing and jockeying for position. Earnest feeding usually does not begin until the sun sets. Then they quickly move out on branches, taking all the flower buds, often the terminal bud, and

VARIATIONS IN NUTRITIONAL VALUE OF GROUSE FOODS

After watching ruffed grouse use the various foods available to them over a period of years, I have some doubts about the value of some of the items that are "popular" foods. Clover is often considered to be an important fall food for ruffed grouse, and establishment of clover on logging trails and other disturbed sites is frequently included in ruffed grouse management prescriptions.

I've certainly seen grouse crops filled with clover leaves, but I question clover's value to ruffed grouse. Over the years, we have seen minimal evidence of use of nearby clover patches by long-surviving males established on drumming logs. Once in a while, we'll see an old bird feeding on clover, but most of the use seems to be by inexperienced young birds. Clover patches clearly provide places where grouse mortality is accelerated, both from predation and hunter-harvest.

In many parts of the ruffed grouse range, fruits and berries are ranked as important foods. Apple orchards have long been considered the place to find ruffed grouse during the fall in New England. But again, I question whether this use is due to availability, and possibly taste, rather than fulfilling a life-sustaining need. The periods when ruffed grouse have made extensive use of fruits and berries at Cloquet have generally been the periods when the grouse population was in difficulty and declining. In northern Minnesota, at least, fruits appear to represent an emergency food or perhaps "dessert," taken by ruffed grouse having difficulty finding more sustaining foods to eat. A fruit diet does not appear suitable for a high-density, productive ruffed grouse population. At Cloquet, we have several patches of crabapple, thorn-apple, dogwood, and mountain-ash that are heavily used by ruffed grouse each fall, but all of these patches are in areas where breeding grouse are especially sparse the next spring.

I suspect some of these "favorite" foods of ruffed grouse should really be considered "junk" foods. They are tasty, abundant, and easily fed upon, but don't provide essential nutrients in the quantity needed by ruffed grouse to survive the winter.

The lesser value of these food items is partly due to the relative amount of food grouse can process on a daily basis. A crop full of clover or strawberry leaves seldom weighs more than 30 to 40 grams, a crop full of thornapples or mountain-ash berries weighs 40 to 60 grams, while a crop full of aspen flower buds may weigh as much as 100 grams. On the basis of nutritional value per meal, as represented by a filled crop, there is quite a difference among these foods.

The grouse's diet has been cited as the reason why a lack of food should not be considered as a factor limiting their distribution or abundance.

I disagree with this assessment. I believe that ruffed grouse are really specialists. They do best when they have a winter-long abundance of one food resource: aspen flower buds. But they can persist fairly well when hazel catkins, willow buds, and perhaps birch and ironwood catkins are available.

Ruffed grouse survive on other diets but at densities that seem to always be well below those found where the grouse have aspen available. On their primary range when aspen buds are not available, for whatever reason, ruffed grouse populations start declining toward the densities prevailing in the marginal regions where aspen is never or seldom available.

The male aspen bud is relatively rich in protein, fats and minerals. The female flower bud is, by stark contrast, nutrient-poor and seldom used by grouse.

perhaps a bit of the twig tip as well. Sometimes all the feeding will be confined to one or two trees, but at other times the birds may eat their way through the tops of several trees.

Most of the feeding in aspen is done in the uppermost branches. Several studies of aspen flower buds have shown that the buds on the uppermost twigs are the largest and most nutritious [14,37,38]. During the years when ruffed grouse numbers are high, a "browse line" begins to appear in the upper one-third of the crowns of preferred aspens as the grouse strip the choice buds from the upper branches. In northern Minnesota, this was particularly evident in 1971 and 1972.

It is often quite dark by time the evening meal is completed and the birds fly into a burrow-roost. This pattern of behavior has its benefits. If it has been warm enough during the day to melt the surface of the snow, the crust will have formed before the grouse completes its evening meal and dives for a snow-burrow. When this happens, a grouse may be shaken-up when it hits the crusted snow, but that is far better than becoming trapped because the bird dived into the snow *before* the crust hardened.

These grouse are quite selective concerning the trees they'll use for feeding. They seldom feed in aspens less than 30-years old, and most of the favored trees are affected by some problem which evidently is reducing their vigor. The tree may be infected by one of the pathogenic fungi (hypoxlyn, nectria, etc.), damaged mechanically or by fire, or simply growing on a site where aspen does not belong. As a rule, trees that are living under stress produce a greater abundance of flowers and fruits than healthier trees, and this is true of aspens, too. When their longevity is in doubt, trees expend a greater effort to pass their genes on to another generation. At Cloquet, the rate of mortality among aspens used frequently for feeding by grouse has been higher than among aspens of the same age but not used by grouse as feeding sites [21].

One of the problems confronting ruffed grouse as a result of their dependence upon aspen is the variability in flower bud production from one

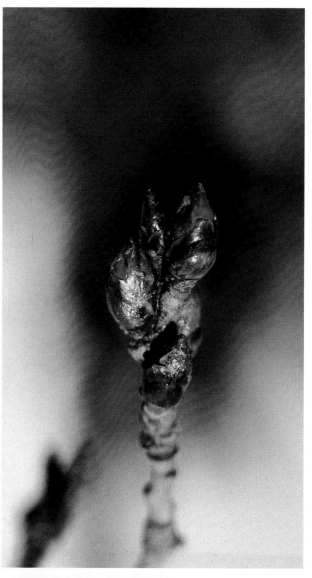

*After sunset the birds quickly move out on
the branches, taking all the buds. Most aspen
feeding is done in the uppermost branches
where the buds are largest and most nutritious.*

year to another. In Minnesota, we have
developed an index to express the relative year-
to-year abundance of these buds. This index is
derived from the average number of buds on each
aspen twig and the percentage of twigs having
flower buds, and is based on trees that we know
ruffed grouse have used for feeding. Some years
that index value may be as high as 293, and a
year or two later as low as 35. The bud supply is
ample when this value exceeds 150, but ruffed
grouse in Minnesota are in trouble when it falls
much below that value.

To complicate matters further, there have
been some seasons when the aspens at Cloquet
identified as preferred feeding trees produced
very few flower buds, while trees in other nearby
clones had an ample supply. This was especially
noticeable in 1980, when we were collecting buds

for some nutrient studies. We needed at least 25
grams of buds from each tree. We had no problem finding that many buds on felled trees with
no history of use, but were unable to collect a sufficient number of buds from some of the trees that
we knew had been used for feeding.

Where aspen is not available to ruffed grouse,
for whatever reason, they will turn to the catkins
of other trees or shrubs. Often, these are trees or
shrubs belonging to the birch family,
(Betulaceae) which include the birches, ironwood, and filbert or hazel. In Eastern forests,
black cherry buds are often important. At one
time, ruffed grouse feeding on apple buds in New
England orchards prompted setting a bounty on
them in some parts of Massachusetts [12].

A person does not have to spend much time
watching grouse feeding on these alternative food

Throughout winter, grouse normally feed twice a day. Bitter cold weather may pre-empt morning feeding, but the evening meal is always taken.

items to realize the advantage of the aspens. Both ironwood and birch have the catkins at the end of long, slender twigs, so grouse feeding on these catkins fly from branch to branch and do much wing fluttering to maintain their balance. This not only means more energy expended, but the commotion also attracts the attention of predators. In return for this effort, they obtain only one, two, or at most, three catkins. Two birch catkins may equal the volume of an aspen bud, but it would take at least three or four ironwood catkins to equal a single aspen flower bud.

Grouse feeding extensively upon these substitute food items in Minnesota do not survive as well as when they are feeding upon the aspen flower buds. When we see grouse making heavy winter use of members of the birch family, we expect to find fewer grouse in the spring, and the weights of surviving birds decline. This all results in decreased drumming activity in the spring, reduced nesting activity, poor production of young grouse, and consequently poorer hunting in the fall.

The differences in the value of foods which grouse use appear to be other than the differences in nutrient levels, since they all are relatively equivalent in available protein, fats, and carbohydrates. It is probably the differences in the amount of other materials present which interfere with the digestive processes in the bird's gut that are important [11]. These materials appear to be phenolic and tannin compounds which may vary in concentrations from plant species to species and probably from year to year.

So how does this variation in the character of food resources affect ruffed grouse numbers? As I perceive this matter, it operates through several interacting effects which are variable enough from year to year to make it difficult to point to a single factor that is consistently responsible.

But the underlying effect that sets the stage is a lower quality food resource, which means that each grouse must take in and process more food to obtain the same amount of energy. That means that each bird must spend more time feeding, and therein lies the crux of the problem. First, if they are not feeding on aspen, they are feeding on a food resource that is not only more expensive to obtain in terms of energy expenditure, but also less rewarding on a per-bite basis.

We have seen no evidence of ruffed grouse starving, but the effect is more subtle than that. Predation is the cause of most mortality for most grouse, but losses from normal levels of predation (55 percent from fall to spring) can be easily replaced by normal levels of production each spring. However, if fall-to-spring losses rise to 65 or 70 percent due to grouse spending too much time feeding, then normal production will not compensate for these losses.

Poor winter-long snow-roosting conditions further exacerbates the problem. Under these conditions, the daily energy requirements of the grouse rise, due to its need to burn energy to keep

Evening feeding on mountain-ash berries, aspen flower buds, and hazel catkins.

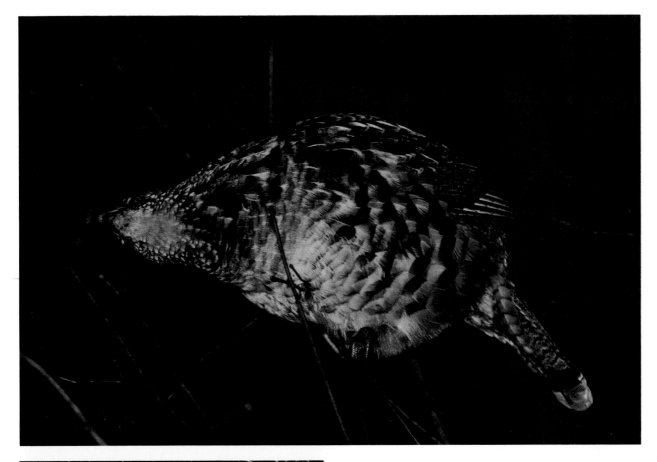

*During winter grouse have little access to grit
— and apparently little need of it.*

warm. This imposes a need for more extended feeding periods, thus increased heat loss to the environment as well as exposure to predation. Also, the birds denied the use of snow-burrows run a much higher risk of predation, as noted earlier. So, they are placed in double jeopardy.

This whole combination of events also means that the surviving grouse are gradually deteriorating physically as the winter wears on so that when they reach spring and the breeding season, they don't have the energy reserves -- nor the desire -- to engage in breeding. So even if overwinter losses have only been normal, the population sags due to failure to replace whatever losses have occurred. If predation losses have been heavy, due either to an influx of northern raptors or to unsatisfactory snow-roosting conditions, the grouse population declines sharply as it did in 1963, 1972-73, and again in 1981-82.

Ruffed grouse and other wildlife are not unlike humans in their willingness to feed on things that may taste good or are abundant but not very nutritious. Just as we have our "junk foods," ruffed grouse feeding heavily upon clover leaves and various berries in the fall appear to be on a junk-food diet. As winter approaches, these birds should be concentrating on foods rich in important nutrients that will be available to them after snow covers the ground.

Although berries are often abundant and grouse feed avidly upon them, those birds are really consuming a considerable amount of water

and comparatively little of the nutrients that prepare them for the winter. Clover leaves are 84 percent water, so a meal of 40 grams of clover leaves provides only 2.8 grams of carbohydrates, 0.2 grams of fat, and 1.6 grams of protein. Generally, berries are composed of 60 percent water and relatively less of the fats, carbohydrates, and proteins they really need. A crop having 60 grams of thornapple fruit contains only 0.8 grams of fat, 13 grams of carbohydrates, and only 0.6 grams of protein. By contrast, when a grouse consumes 100 grams of male aspen flower buds, it has eaten 6.5 grams of fats, 14 grams of carbohydrates, and about 6.4 grams of protein.[38]

One of the interesting differences among the families of the Galliformes is the matter of fat storage. Pheasants, quail, partridges, and many other birds store fat during the fall to provide reserves for the long migration flight south or the winter ahead. Grouse, as a rule, store little fat, counting on having ample food resources available on a day-to-day basis throughout the winter [45,72]. Since the grouse's primary food resources are in the trees and shrubs above the snow, this has been a successful strategy.

Ruffed grouse are not alone in their use of aspen flower buds. In Minnesota, sharptailed grouse feed on aspen buds too, and at least occasionally, both evening grosbeaks and purple finches consume these buds. In the Western mountains, a close relative of purple finches, the Cassin's finch, is at least as dependent as ruffed grouse upon aspen buds [65].

Black bears fresh out of hibernation climb the trees to feed on the extended catkins [62]. And, just as ruffed grouse have clearly shown a preference for feeding in certain aspens, bears climb some aspens more frequently than others.

Ruffed grouse, like other members of the family Tetraonidae (and deer, moose, elk, and other ungulates), depend upon a symbiotic relationship with micro-organisms for handling the digestion of many of the things they eat. They crush their food in a muscular gizzard, mix it with digestive juices to produce a "chyme," and then pass this mixture into a long, paired, blind

By late autumn the birds that have forsaken aspen for "junk food" items are probably in trouble when snow covers these resources.

gut, or "ceca." There, the micro-organisms break down the complex plant celluloses, lignins, and other materials into simpler chemicals that grouse can absorb and use.

This is important to an understanding of how and why some plants are important as food for ruffed grouse, and why other seemingly useful plants are of little or no value.

Recent research by Dr. John Bryant and his associates in Alaska has provided a basis for evaluating fall and winter feeding activities somewhat differently than we have done in the past [11]. Dr. Bryant's work has identified certain chemicals that are sometimes present in the food of herbivores which inhibit the activities of the micro-organisms.

One example of the effect of this chemical inhibition is the lack of use of alder catkins. These appear to be an attractive and certainly are an abundant food resource in many grouse habitats. But Bryant's study suggests that the alder catkin has a very high tannin content. In Minnesota, it is rare to see ruffed grouse feeding in alder, even where it is one of the most abundant shrubs in grouse habitat. It appears likely that a high tannin content in alder catkins interferes with the ability of ruffed grouse to metabolize this abundant food.

Another side of this story is the old, familiar story of conditioning, or adaptation of the gut micro-organisms to a changed diet. This has long been recognized as the primary reason why emergency, late-winter feeding of hay to deer seldom saves many of the starving animals. Deer eat the food, but they don't have enough of the right micro-organisms in their stomachs to handle the food. So, many deer die with their bellies full of high-quality hay.

The ruffed grouse story seems to be similar. The birds that are most likely to survive after the berries are gone and snow buries the succulent leaves of the low growing, frost-resistant herbs, are the grouse that began feeding on aspen flower buds or hazel and birch catkins early in the fall. By beginning this pattern of feedng long before they are forced to, these birds are developing or conditioning a population of cecal micro-

organisms that will be abundant enough to handle these foods when only they are available.

At Cloquet, a radio-tagged, 14-week old ruffed grouse was recorded feeding on aspen flower buds as early as September 30th [19]. By mid-October, it is common to find many grouse feeding more heavily on aspen flower buds or hazel catkins than on berries or succulent, herbaceous greenery. But many grouse still continue to feed on these tastier items, and it is probable that these birds are in trouble once those food resources are covered with snow.

In the first chapter, we said we'd present another hypothesis as to why ruffed grouse numbers fluctuate so widely in some parts of their range and so little in other regions. This hypothesis is based on observations of grouse making heavy use of aspen flower buds some years, but little or no use of them during other winters. Sometimes the latter has been the case even when there was an abundance of flower buds on the same aspens that had been heavily used in previous seasons.

Early on, the interpretation of these observations was puzzling, for grouse were making heavy use of the extended catkins in April, even though they had not eaten the buds during the winter.

Some years ago, we had concluded that something on the bud scales must be interfering with grouse use of the buds, for once the catkins had emerged in the spring, we knew grouse could take those without ingesting the bud scales. Having handled aspen buds earlier, we knew the buds were covered with a gummy resin. In fact, buds of the closely related balsam-poplar have such a heavy coating of a gummy resin that we seldom see ruffed grouse taking these buds, although they feed on the extended catkins.

Dr. Bryant has identified a phenol component in this resin on the aspen buds which appears to inhibit the activity of the micro-organisms in the bird's gut. Grouse feeding on buds covered with the resin containing this phenol would have difficulty digesting them.

A hypothesis develops from combining this information with the knowledge that the regions where ruffed grouse show the most dramatic fluctuations are those parts of their range where winter food resources are limited to aspen and perhaps two or three other foods such as willows, birch, and hazel. The hypothesis is that periodic changes in the chemistry of aspen flower buds is an underlying cause for the ruffed grouse cycles.

This is not a new idea. J. Burton Laukhart, a Washington State game biologist proposed the idea that variations in food quality were related to wildlife cycles in 1957, but his idea has not been given much serious consideration [47]. In part, this was because few people interested in these phenomena believed that food resources might at times limit ruffed grouse abundance.

There are still aspects of the story that we don't understand. For example, why did grouse have a long period when they enjoyed unrestricted use of aspen flower buds from 1965 to 1971, and their numbers soared to the highest level seen in northern Minnesota since the early 1950s? But then, they were unable to use aspen from 1973 to 1975, but did make use of it again in 1976 and 1977, but not from 1978 to 1983. Grouse numbers started up sharply in the 1976-77 period, when aspen was being used, but stagnated in 1978 and remained relatively static until 1981. Then the population began a slump, and by 1983 had reached the lowest level seen since the mid-1960s.

The overriding question, if this hypothesis is valid, is why do the aspens allow their buds to be eaten in some years and not in others? What is the mechanism that triggers the trees into producing the materials that render their flower buds chemically unavailable?

In 1972, we saw much evidence of excessive browsing on aspen by ruffed grouse. Some heavily-used trees were not only stripped of flower buds but suffered an estimated 40 to 60 percent loss of the terminal buds necessary to produce leaves and twigs. This damage was even more severe than that inflicted by a tent caterpillar ("army-worm") infestation. But overbrowsing by grouse was not evident in 1977-78 when the aspen were "turned-off" again. So while there is good reason to suspect a close relationship between the chemistry of aspen flower buds and ruffed grouse cycles, the big question still remains, why?

Chapter Eleven

PREDATION

Ruffed grouse are at the bottom of the food chain, the "energy pyramid." They are "primary consumers," that is, ruffed grouse feed primarily on plants and convert plant materials into animal protein. In this way, they provide a source of energy for many other animals higher in the food chain. In the biological scheme of things, ruffed grouse are designed to be eaten. Some 400,000 to 1.25 million pounds of grouse are harvested for human consumption in Minnesota annually, and across the continent, this amounts to almost eight million pounds of meat. This is only a fraction of the grouse that sustain the lives of other animals.

When snow lies heavily across the countryside in northern Minnesota, there are only three animals sufficiently abundant and large enough to feed the larger hawks and owls that live in this region. Ruffed grouse share with snowshoe hares and red squirrels this role in the lives of horned owls, great gray owls, barred owls, and goshawks.

Among the raptors, the great gray owl is probably the only one that is fairly effective at taking grouse concealed in a snow-burrow. While studying a resident population of great gray owls in northcentral Minnesota, Steve Loch found that great gray owls could evidently hear grouse in their snow-burrows and successfully prey upon the concealed birds. This seems to be a trait unique to these owls. Fortunately for North Shore ruffed grouse, great gray owls are not that common.

The only other predator that is fairly proficient in taking ruffed grouse from snow-burrows is the lynx. This subarctic cat has large feet and can move stealthily over soft snow, enabling it to find grouse that are securely hidden from other, less adept, predators.

The relative importance of these prey species to the various predators varies from year to year. The seasons when there are large numbers of inexperienced young ruffed grouse in the woods, and snowshoe hares are scarce, grouse are a more important source of winter-long nutrition. When grouse are scarce and hares are abundant, the opposite is true.

The relative level of predation also varies depending upon winter snow conditions. If deep, soft snow persists all winter, providing ideal burrowing conditions for ruffed grouse, snowshoe hares are subjected to heavy predation. If the snow is hard-crusted and grouse are unable to burrow-roost, the all-white snowshoe hares have the advantage.

Other factors also have a bearing on the severi-

CLOSE CALLS

Not all ruffed grouse that predators capture are killed and eaten. We have encountered varying numbers of "near misses" among drumming males handled each spring.

Grouse 900, probably the first bird on Earth to carry a radio-transmitter, had a very close call six months earlier. A predator had restrained him long enough to pluck the right side of his tail and four primary flight feathers from his right wing.

In April 1964, I found where another male was captured by a fox. The trail of feathers led into a lowland bog where it was lost, but enough feathers were recovered to be certain that the drummer resident in this center since 1962 had been taken. But the bird escaped, returned to his log later in 1964, and continued as an active drummer until a raptor caught him in 1967.

Another bird that escaped after considerable mauling by a predator was handled in 1978. The evening before we trapped this male, he was flushed out of aspens overhead, and we could clearly hear his bands jingling on his legs as he flew. As he flew, we also knew he had a problem. The next morning we found out what it was. He, too, had lost most of his tail and the three outermost primaries on his left wing.

Among the North Shore raptors, great gray owls are fairly effective at taking grouse in snow-burrows. A study indicates that the owls may actually hear the burrowed grouse.

The hunters . . .

. . . and the hunted.

Goshawks evidently take grouse whenever the opportunity arises. If they don't immediately consume their prey, it may be cached in a tree for later use.

A brown grouse contrasted against the snow is an easy target for predators.

Ruffed grouse are an important segment of the North Shore prey population and few perish gently. Virtually all of them will die as a meal for another animal.

ty of predation and its effect upon a grouse population. Predation upon grouse is minimized in the years when they are able to feed on aspen flower buds and spend a minimal amount of time in exposed situations. If they must feed on less satisfactory food materials and spend more time in the tops of birches or climbing around in the hazel brush, their vulnerability to predation becomes much greater, even if they have good roosting snow. There are a number of factors which affect the impact of predators upon a grouse population.

Certainly ruffed grouse are an important part of the prey population on the North Shore. Few grouse perish gently.

In those years when conditions are particularly favorable for ruffed grouse, and snowshoe hares are scarce, predators may suffer considerably,

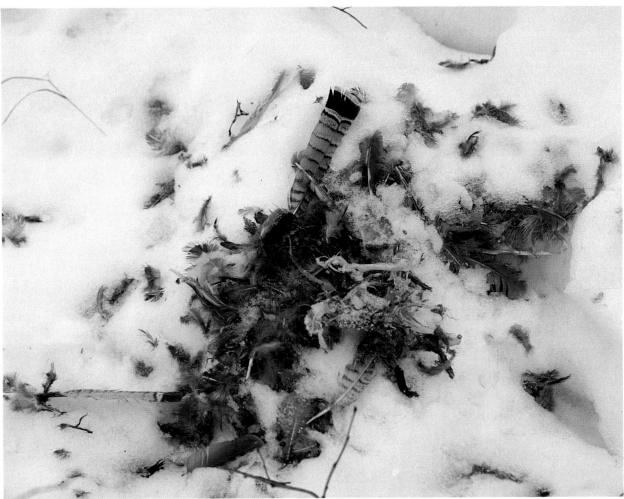

We have at times found more evidence of predation upon predators than grouse! When prey species are scarce, large raptors may begin feeding upon the smaller ones.

and much "interpredation" (predation by predators upon other predators) occurs. Great horned owls and goshawks prey upon barred owls, and horned owls prey upon goshawks, as the larger eats the smaller. At Cloquet, ruffed grouse and snowshoe hares were quite scare in 1965, and winter snow conditions very favorable. That spring, we found that predators ate each other more often than they dined on grouse. Barred owls were the primary prey species.

Hawks and owls are the major predators upon ruffed grouse for most of the year. Among the raptors, the goshawk is surely the most efficient of all. Once a grouse has attracted the attention of a goshawk, it is probably seldom that the grouse survives. A goshawk will even land on the ground and pursue a grouse through heavy cover on foot. But goshawks have difficulty pursuing ruffed grouse flying through sapling stands which

is why this type of stand is considered secure grouse cover.

Goshawks are especially adept at taking advantage of the screening effect of evergreen foliage. This allows them to remain concealed until an unsuspecting grouse moves into a vulnerable position on the forest floor. This ability by goshawks and other raptors to exploit the value of the year-around screening cover of the conifers is one reason why grouse numbers on the North Shore are consistently lower than in other parts of Minnesota where coniferous cover is less prevalent.

The goshawk is sufficiently efficient as a predator upon ruffed grouse that it could appropriately be called the "grouse-hawk," for there surely is no other animal as adept in its pursuit of this bird. Fortunately, goshawks are uncommon in most regions. For many people, the

Even the swift and graceful goshawk is not safe from untimely death. Weakened from poor hunting and hunger, it may risk an attack on a grouse in dense cover.

thrill of seeing a live goshawk is a greater treat then seeing ruffed grouse.

On the Cloquet Forest, we have been especially fortunate from the research point of view to have had nesting goshawks present for a large portion of the past quarter-century. We believe that a pair of goshawks kill on the order of 270 to 315 ruffed grouse annually on this five-square-mile forest [29].

Goshawks evidently kill whenever the opportunity occurs. If they don't eat their prey at the time it is killed, they may cache it for later on. But occasionally, goshawks make mistakes too. Catching a foot in the fork of a branch is only one of the accidents that can befall this boldest of predators.

The history of goshawk activity on the Cloquet Forest has provided a unique opportunity to document the importance of the forest composi-

tion. On those areas where the raptors have the advantage of conifer cover, spring breeding densities of ruffed grouse are in the order of 5.6 to 7.8 birds per 100 acres, but in those areas where grouse can live in suitably-dense aspen sapling stands, breeding ruffed grouse numbers reach densities of 44 birds/100 acres.

The effectiveness of goshawk predation upon a ruffed grouse population was dramatically illustrated on the Cloquet Forest in 1978. Goshawks had not nested on the forest since 1967, and ruffed grouse had moved into many conifer-dominated sites. This created a bonanza for a pair of goshawks when they decided to nest again on the Cloquet Forest. At least 47 drumming males were occupying drumming logs within a one-mile radius of the goshawk nest in the spring of 1978. By mid-June of that year, this pair of goshawks had taken at least 23 percent of

*After working with ruffed grouse for a quarter
century, I guess I am most impressed by just how little
we still really know about these birds, and how they
cope with all the problems they must face daily.*

these drumming males.

Significantly, most of those grouse were taken from the area where pines provided the raptors with good concealment. From 1978 to 1983, the breeding grouse population in that area declined from 2.68 to 0.22 males/100 acres [33].

Although goshawks can be deadly when conditions favor them, ruffed grouse can be secure even when goshawks are present if cover conditions are right.

In recent years, there have been two major invasions of goshawks moving down from the north. In 1972, 5,382 goshawks were counted as they moved down the North Shore by Duluth's Hawk Ridge [61]. This contrasts with the usual year when a few dozen up to 300 goshawks are counted. In the winter of 1972-73, there were virtually no flower buds on the aspen in this region, and there were only eight days of snow adequate for burrow-roosting. This shortage of food combined with inadequate snow cover made ruffed grouse especially vulnerable. The influx of goshawks and other raptors from the subarctic resulted in heavy predation, with only 31 percent of the breeding male grouse surviving from 1972 to 1973 at Cloquet.

In 1982, 5,819 goshawks were counted at Hawk Ridge, but conditions were more in favor of grouse. Although the food supply was poor in 1982-83, snow-roosting conditions were favorable for at least 46 days. In spite of the considerable influx of goshawks, 46 percent of the breeding males survived from 1982 to 1983.

Even though goshawks are especially efficient predators upon ruffed grouse, they are generally too scarce to be the major predator across most of the latter's range. The great horned owl must be given credit for this role. Horned owls are likely to be resident in just about any forest area supporting a grouse population.

Although the raptors are by far the most important predators upon fully-grown ruffed grouse in northern forests, a number of other animals will certainly kill a grouse, given the opportunity. But I don't believe any other predators are as dependent upon ruffed grouse as are the larger, wintering raptors. At Cloquet, of 584 predator kills examined where the species responsible could be determined, 86 percent were attributed to raptor predation; 49 percent of those were known or believed to be goshawk kills.

Identifying the predator responsible for making a kill is usually difficult, often deceiving, and sometimes impossible. Once a friend who always insisted that foxes were the most important predators upon ruffed grouse here told me with some delight about the kill of a banded grouse he had just found. When I examined the site, there was no question about a fox being involved. There were tracks all over the snow and a few crushed bones. But digging in the snow to recover another band that I could see deeper, I uncovered the tell-tale, chalky "whites" so often deposited by raptors while they are feeding. The verdict was that a goshawk made the kill and probably left enough meat on the bones to attract the fox that scavenged the remains.

Another time, I saw where a grouse had been taken in flight by a raptor and together they dropped into fresh snow. The raptor probably killed the grouse where they fell, but before it was able to feast on it, a fox came along, took the grouse from the raptor, carried it a short distance, and ate it. If the snow had not been fresh, that kill would have been attributed to the fox.

We also know that barred owls can readily take ruffed grouse. On a February evening in 1961, I released a banded female grouse from a trap. Although I knew a barred owl was perched in a tall red pine overhead, I did not believe the owl was a threat to this grouse once it was releas-

ed. I was wrong. Although the grouse had a 50 yard head start, the owl overtook the grouse about 300 feet from the release site and ate her there. To prove this was not an isolated incident, at this site the owl regurgitated a pellet containing the skull and other parts of another grouse it had eaten earlier.

IN CONCLUSION!

I want to close this story about ruffed grouse on the North Shore by saying that these birds are fascinating animals to work with. Each individual grouse is as different as each individual human, and while we can generalize about how they do things, there are almost always exceptions to the rules. After working with them for a quarter-century, I guess I am most impressed by just how little we still really do know about these birds and how they cope with all the problems they must face daily.

I believe we have a pretty sound basis now for prescribing the types of woodland management that is most beneficial to them. But economic pressures may often impede our ability to execute these plans. On the other hand, I suspect the underlying causes for their periodic cycles are beyond our control. We may be able to do things that dampen the severity of those cycles, but I suspect that for as long as ruffed grouse live in our northern regions, they will appear to be moving towards extinction about every 10 years, but become moderately to truly plentiful four or five years later.

THE END

APPENDIX

APPENDIX
Plants and Animals Mentioned in the Text

BIRDS
Capercaillie *Tetrao urogallus*

Chukar *Alectoris chukar*

Crossbills *Loxia* sp.

Crow *Corvus brachyrhynchos*

Finch, Cassin's *Carpodacus cassinii*

Finch, purple *Carpodacus purpureus*

Flicker *Colaptes auratus*

Goshawk *Accipiter gentilis*

Grosbeak, evening *Coccothraustes vespertinus*

Grosbeak, pine *Pinicola enucleator*

Grouse, black *Lyrurus tetrix*

Grouse, black-breasted hazel *Bonasa sewerzowi*

Grouse, blue *Dendragapus obscurus*

Grouse, hazel *Bonasa bonasia*

Grouse, red *Lagopus lagopus scoticus*

Grouse, ruffed *Bonasa umbellus*

Grouse, sage *Centrocercus urophasianus*

Grouse, sharp-tailed *Tympanuchus phasianellus*

Grouse, spruce *Dendragapus canadensis*

Hawk, broad-winged *Buteo platypterus*

Hawk, Cooper's *Accipiter cooperii*

Hawk, sharp-shinned *Accipiter striatus*

Jay, blue *Cyanocitta cristata*

Owl, barred *Strix varia*

Owl, great gray *Strix nebulosa*

Owl, great horned *Bubo virginianus*

Partridge, gray *Perdix perdix*

Prairie-chicken, greater (pinnated grouse)
   Tympanuchus cupido

Ptarmigan, rock *Lagopus mutus*

Ptarmigan, white-tailed *Lagopus leucurus*

Ptarmigan, willow *Lagopus lagopus*

Redpoll *Carduelis flammea*

Robin *Turdus migratorius*

Waxwing *Bombycilla cedrorum*

Woodcock *Scolopax minor*

MAMMALS
Bear, black *Ursus americanus*

Bobcat *Lynx rufus*

Chipmunks *Tamias* spp.

Coyote *Canus latrans*

Deer, white-tailed *Odocoileus virginianus*

Elk *Cervus elaphus*
Fox, red *Vulpes vulpes*
Hare, snowshoe *Lepus americanus*
Lynx *Lynx canadensis*
Moose *Alces alces*
Porcupine *Erethizon dorsatum*
Raccoon *Procyon lotor*
Skunk *Mephitis mephitis*
Squirrel, fox *Sciurus niger*
Squirrel, gray *Sciurus carolinensis*
Squirrel, red *Tamiasciurus hudsonicus*
Weasels *Mustela spp.*
Woodchuck *Marmota monax*

PLANTS

Alder *Alnus incana*
Anemone *Anemone quinquefolia*
Aspen, big-tooth *Populus grandidentata*
Aspen, quaking *Populus tremuloides*
Bearberry *Arctostaphlos uva-ursi*
Birch, paper *Betula papyrifera*
Blueberries *Vaccinium* spp.
Bunchberry *Cornus canadensis*
Cedar, white *Thuja occidentalis*
Cherry, black *Prunus serotina*
Cherry, choke *Prunus virginiana*
Cherry, pin *Prunus pensylvanica*
Clover *Trifolium* spp.
Cottonwood, black *Populus trichocarpa*
Cranberry, highbush *Viburnum trilobum*

Dogwood, gray *Cornus racemosa*
False lily-of-the-valley *Maianthemum candense*
Fern, bracken *Pteridium aguilinum*
Fir, balsam *Abies balsamea*
Goldthread *Coptis groenlandica*
Hazel (filbert) *Corylus cornuta*
Hemlock *Tsuga canadensis*
Hepatica *Hepatica americana*
Hophornbeam (ironwood) *Ostrya virginiana*
Juneberry *Amelanchier* spp.
Maple *Acer* spp.
Maple, red *Acer rubrum*
Marshmarigold *Caltha palustris*
Milkwort *Polygala* sp.
Mountain-ash *Sorbus* spp.
Oak *Quercus* spp.
Pine, jack *Pinus banksiana*
Pine, red *Pinus resinosa*
Poplar, balsam *Populus balsamifera*
Raspberry *Rubus* spp.
Rose *Rosa* spp.
Sarsaparilla *Aralia nudicaulis*
Sedges *Carex* spp.
Springbeauty *Claytonia* spp.
Spruce *Picea* spp.
Spruce, black *Picea mariana*
Strawberries *Fragaria* spp.
Tamarack *Larix laricina*
Thornapple *Crataegus* spp.
Trailing-arbutus *Epigaea repens*

BIBLIOGRAPHY

1. Aldrich, J.W. 1963. Geographic orientation of American Tetraonidae. Journal of Wildlife Management, 27:529-545.

2. Archibald, H.L. 1973. Spring drumming activity and space use of ruffed grouse. Ph.D. Thesis, University of Minnesota, Minneapolis.

3. Backs, S.E. 1984. Ruffed grouse restoration in Indiana. *In* W.L. Robinson, ed., Proceedings of the Ruffed Grouse Management Symposium, 45th Midwest Fish & Wildlife Conference. (in press).

4. Bailey, W.J., Jr., W.M. Sharp, R.B. Hazel, and G. Davis. 1955. Food habit trends of ruffed grouse in the Centre County "Barrens." Pennsylvania State University, Agricultural Experiment Station Bulletin 604.

5. Barrett, R.W. 1970. Behavior of ruffed grouse during the breeding and early brood rearing periods. Ph.D. Thesis, University of Minnesota, Minneapolis.

6. Bergmann, H.H., S. Klaus, F. Muller, and J. Wisener. 1978. Das haselhuhn. A. Ziemsen Verlag, Wittenberg Lutherstadt.

7. Bezdek, H. 1944. Sex ratios and color phases in two races of ruffed grouse. Journal of Wildlife Management, 8:85-88.

8. Brander, R.B. 1965. Factors affecting dispersion of ruffed grouse during late winter and spring on the Cloquet Forest Research Center, Minnesota. Ph.D. Thesis, University of Minnesota, Minneapolis.

9. Brewer, L.W. 1980. The ruffed grouse in western Washington. Washington Department of Game, Biological Bulletin No. 16.

10. Brown, C.P. 1946. Food of Maine ruffed grouse by seasons and cover types. Journal of Wildlife Management, 10:17-28.

11. Bryant, J.P. and P.J. Kuropat. 1980. Selection of winter forage by subarctic browsing vertebrates: the role of plant

chemistry. Annual Review of Ecological Systems, 11:261-285.

12. Bump, G., R.W. Darrow, F.C. Edminster, and W.F. Crissey. 1947. The ruffed grouse: life history - propagation -management. New York Conservation Department, Albany.

13. Davis, J.A. 1969. Aging and sexing criteria for Ohio ruffed grouse. Journal of Wildlife Management, 33:628-636.

14. Doerr, P.D., L.B. Keith, D.H. Rusch, and C.A. Fisher. 1974. Characteristics of winter feeding aggregations of ruffed grouse in Alberta. Journal of Wildlife Management, 38:601-615.

15. Eng, R.L. 1959. A study of the ecology of male ruffed grouse *(Bonasa umbellus L.)* on the Cloquet Forest Research Center, Minnesota. Ph.D. Thesis, University of Minnesota, Minneapolis.

16. Fisher, L.W. 1939. Studies of the eastern ruffed grouse in Michigan. Michigan State University, Agricultural Experiment Station, Technical Bulletin 166.

17. Formozov, A.N. 1964. Snow cover as an integral factor of the environment and its importance in the ecology of birds and mammals. Boreal Institute, University of Alberta, Occasional Paper No. 1. (Transl. by W. Prychodko and W.O. Pruitt, Jr.)

18. Garbutt, A.S. and A.L.A. Middleton. [n.d.] The rearing and maintenance of ruffed grouse, *Bonasa umbellus,* in captivity. Department of Zoology, University of Guelph, Guelph, Ontario.

19. Godfrey, G.A. 1967. Summer and fall movements and behavior of immature ruffed grouse. *(Bonasa umbellus* (L.)).

M.S. Thesis, University of Minnesota, Minneapolis.

20. Godfrey, G.A. and W.H. Marshall. 1969. Brood break-up and dispersal of ruffed grouse. Journal of Wildlife Management, 33:609-620.

21. Gottlieb, G. 1971. Development of species identification in birds: an inquiry into the prenatal determinants of perception. University of Chicago Press, Chicago.

22. Greeley, F.C. 1975. Popple partridge. Massachusetts Wildlife, Sept.-Oct. 1975.

23. Greenwood, C.J. 1977. The effects of auditory and selected environmental stimuli on hatching synchrony in ruffed grouse *(Bonasa umbellus* Linnaeus). M.S. Thesis, University of Guelph, Guelph, Ontario.

24. Gullion, G.W. 1966. A viewpoint concerning the significance of studies of game bird food habits. Condor, 68:372-376.

25. Gullion, G.W. 1966. The use of drumming behavior in ruffed grouse population studies. Journal of Wildlife Management, 30:717-729.

26. Gullion, G.W. 1970. Factors influencing ruffed grouse populations. P. 93-105 *in* Transactions 35th North American Wildlife & Natural Resources Conference.

27. Gullion, G.W. 1981. Non-drumming males in a ruffed grouse population. Wilson Bulletin, 93:372-382.

28. Gullion, G.W. 1981. A quarter century of goshawk nesting at Cloquet. Loon 53:3-5.

29. Gullion, G.W. 1981. The impact of

goshawk predation upon ruffed grouse. Loon 53:82-84.

30. Gullion, G.W. 1984. Managing northern forests for wildlife. The Ruffed Grouse Society, Coraopolis, PA. (in press).

31. Gullion, G.W. 1984. Ruffed grouse management -- where do we stand in the eighties? *In* W.L. Robinson, ed., Proceedings of the Ruffed Grouse Management Symposium, 45th Midwest Fish & Wildlife Conference. (in press).

32. Gullion, G.W. and W.H. Marshall. 1968. Survival of ruffed grouse in a boreal forest. Living Bird, 7:117-167.

33. Gullion, G.W. and A.A. Alm. 1983. Forest management and ruffed grouse populations in a Minnesota coniferous forest. Journal of Forestry, 81:529-531,536.

34. Hale, P.E., A.S. Johnson, and J.L. Landers. 1982. Characteristics of ruffed grouse drumming sites in Georgia. Journal of Wildlife Management, 46:115-123.

35. Heinselman, M.L. 1973. Fire in the virgin forests of the Boundary Waters Canoe Area, Minnesota. Quarternary Research, 3:329-382.

36. Hoffman, R.W. and C.E. Braun. 1978. Characteristics and status of ruffed grouse and blue grouse in Colorado. Western Birds, 9:121-126.

37. Huempfner, R.A. 1981. Winter arboreal feeding behavior of ruffed grouse in east-central Minnesota. M.S. Thesis, University of Minnesota, Minneapolis.

38. Huff, D.E. 1970. A study of selected nutrients in browse available to the ruffed grouse. M.S. Thesis, University of Minnesota, Minneapolis.

39. Johnsgard, P.A. 1973. Grouse and quails of North America. University of Nebraska Press, Lincoln.

40. Johnsgard, P.A. 1983. The grouse of the world. University of Nebraska Press, Lincoln.

41. Keith, L.B. 1963. Wildlife's ten-year cycle. University of Wisconsin Press, Madison.

42. Kelso, L.H. 1935. Winter food of ruffed grouse in New York. U.S. Department of Agriculture, Bureau of Biological Survey, Wildlife Research & Management Leaflet BS-1.

43. Kubisiak, J.F. 1978. Brood characteristics and summer habitats of ruffed grouse in central Wisconsin. Wisconsin Department of Natural Resources, Technical Bulletin No. 108.

44. Kupa, J.J. 1966. Ecological studies of the female ruffed grouse *(Bonasa umbellus* L.) at the Cloquet Forest Research Center, Minnesota. Ph.D. Thesis, University of Minnesota, Minneapolis.

45. Kuzima, M.A. 1961. Adaptation of Tetraonidae and Phasianidae to climatic conditions. Transactions of the Institute of Zoology, Academy of Science, Kazakh S.S.R., 15:104-114. (translated from the Russian).

46. Landwehr, T.J. (ed.) 1983. Status of wildlife populations, fall 1983 and 1978-1982 hunting and trapping harvest statistics. Minnesota Department of Natural Resources, Section of Wildlife, St. Paul.

47. Lauckhart, J.B. 1957. Animal cycles and food. Journal of Wildlife Management, 21:230-234.

48. Lawson, B.A. 1982. Dichromatism of ruffed grouse and associated meteorological variables. M.S. Thesis, Frostburg State College, Frostburg, MD.

49. Leopold, A. 1933. Game management. Charles Scribners, New York.

50. Maxson, S.J. 1977. Activity patterns of female ruffed grouse during the breeding season. Wilson Bulletin, 89:439-455.

51. Maxson, S.J. 1978. Spring home range and habitat use by female ruffed grouse. Journal of Wildlife Management, 42:61-71.

52. McBurney, R.S. 1970. Drumming behavior of ruffed grouse (Bonasa umbellus (L.)) in Iowa. M.S. Thesis, Iowa State University, Ames.

53. Meslow, E.C. 1966. The drumming log and drumming log activity of male ruffed grouse. M.S. Thesis, University of Minnesota, Minneapolis.

54. Merrill, J.C. 1888. Notes on the birds of Fort Klamath, Oregon. Auk, 5:139-146.

55. Palmer, W.L. and C.L. Bennett, Jr. 1963. Relation of season length to hunting harvest of ruffed grouse. Journal of Wildlife Management, 27:634-639.

56. Petraborg, W.H., E.G. Wellein, and V.E. Gunvalson. 1953. Roadside drumming counts - a spring census method for ruffed grouse. Journal of Wildlife Management, 17:292-295.

57. Phillips, R.L. 1967. Fall and winter food habits of ruffed grouse in northern Utah. Journal of Wildlife Management, 31:827-829.

58. Prawdzik, T.R. 1963. Ruffed grouse escaping a Cooper's hawk. Journal of Wildlife Management, 27:639-642.

59. Pynnonen, A. 1954. Beitrage zur kenntnis der lebensweise des haselhuhns, Tetrastes bonasia (L.). Finnish Game Foundation, Papers on Game Research 12.

60. Rasmussen, G. and R. Brander. 1973. Standard metabolic rate and lower critical temperature for the ruffed grouse. Wilson Bulletin, 85:223-229.

61. Raway, B., ed. 1982. 31-year summary. Duluth Audubon Society, Hawk Ridge Nature Preserve Annual Report, March, 1982.

62. Rogers, L.L. 1977. Social relationships, movements, and population dynamics of black bears in northeastern Minnesota. Ph.D. Thesis, University of Minnesota, Minneapolis.

63. Roussel, Y.E. and R. Ouellet. 1975. A new criterion for sexing Quebec ruffed grouse. Journal of Wildlife Management, 39:443-445.

64. Rusch, D.H. and L.B. Keith. 1971. Seasonal and annual trends in numbers of Alberta ruffed grouse. Journal of Wildlife Management, 35:803-822.

65. Samson, F.B. 1976. Territory, breeding density and fall departure in Cassin's finch. Auk, 93:477-497.

66. Schladweiler, P. 1968. Feeding behavior of incubating ruffed grouse females. Journal of Wildlife Management, 32:426-428.

67. Stoll, R.J., M.W. McClain, C.M. Nixon, and D.M. Worley. 1980. Foods of ruffed grouse in Ohio. Ohio Division of Wildlife, Fish & Wildlife Report 7.

68. Stollberg, B.P. and R.L. Hine. 1952. Food habits studies of ruffed grouse, pheasant, quail and mink in Wisconsin. Wisconsin Conservation Department, Technical Wildlife Bulletin No. 4.

69. Strand, F.C. 1978. A comparison of vegetation characteristics at ruffed grouse drumming logs and predator kill sites. M.S. Plan B Paper, University of Minnesota, Minneapolis.

70. Studer, J.H., ed. 1888. The birds of North America. J.H. Studer Publisher, New York.

71. Svoboda, F.J. and G.W. Gullion.. 1972. Preferential use of aspen by ruffed grouse in northern Minnesota. Journal of Wildlife Management, 36:1166-1180.

72. Thomas, V.G., H.G. Lumsden, and D.H. Price. 1975. Aspects of winter metabolism of ruffed grouse *(Bonasa umbellus)* with special reference to energy reserves. Canadian Journal of Zoology, 53:434-440.

73. Vanderschaegen, P.V. 1970. Food habits of ruffed grouse at the Cloquet Forest Research Center, Minnesota. M.S. Thesis, University of Minnesota, Minneapolis.

74. Veghte, J.H. and C.F. Herreid. 1965. Radiometric determination of feather insulation and metabolism of Arctic birds. Physiological Zoology, 38:267-275.

75. Vince, A.M. 1969. Embryonic communication, respiration and the synchronization of hatching. P.233-260 *in* R.A. Hinde, ed., Bird Vocalizations. Cambridge University Press, London & New York.

76. Wenstrom, W.P., P.V. Vanderschaegen, and G.W. Gullion. 1972. Ruffed grouse primary molt chronology. Auk, 89:671-673.

77. Wetmore, A. 1940. Check-list of the fossil birds of North America. Smithsonian Miscellaneous Collections. 99:1-81.